D1121022

The Balham Group

Cover picture:
Clapham Common,
a Sunday morning in May 1933.
The speaker's platform by the tree.
Hugo Dewar is holding
the Balham Group's first printed paper
the *Red Flag*.
Others, left to right:
Bill Rowlands, Cyril Whiting, Frank Chalcroft,
Temple, Reg Groves (at back) and,
on extreme right, Henry Sara.

The Balham Group

How British Trotskyism Began

Reg Groves

Pluto Press Limited

Also by Reg Groves:

But We Shall Rise Again
A Narrative History of Chartism

The Mystery of Victor Grayson

Rebels' Oak
The Norfolk Rebellion of 1549

The Peasants' Revolt of 1381

Sharpen the Sickle
A History of the Farm Workers' Union

Conrad Noel and the Thaxted Movement

Parts of this book first appeared under the title
'Against the Stream' in *International Socialism*, 54-59.
This edition, with additional material, first published March 1974
by Pluto Press Ltd
Unit 10 Spencer Court, 7 Chalcot Road London NW1 8LH

Copyright © Pluto Press Ltd 1974

ISBN 0 902818 43 0 (hardback)
ISBN 0 902818 42 2 (paperback)

Printed in Great Britain by Bristol Typesetting Company Limited,
Barton Manor, St Philips, Bristol

Designed by Lone Morton

Contents

Come, join in the only battle
wherein no man can fail,
Where whoso fadeth and dieth,
Yet his deed shall still prevail.

Ah! come, cast off all fooling,
for this, at least, we know:
That the Dawn and the Day is coming,
and forth the Banners go.

William Morris

Foreword

This brief chronicle tells of the only struggle within the British Communist Party against that party's final and absolute submission in the years 1929–32 to Stalin and the rulers of Russia. A confused, and certainly hopeless protest, it all happened a long time ago and is now no more than a footnote on the pages of our left socialist histories.

Yet it is right that it should be recorded; and the names remembered of the handful who spoke out against the destruction of true socialism and communism, and who did so when almost everyone else on the Left, especially the intellectuals, remained silent, or cheered on Stalin and the bully boys. And, if personal recollection – with its frayed edges and blurred vision – here takes precedence over such useful things as dates, details and documentation, it is because this can be a warmer way of recalling old friends, and catching sight of them, as it were, in the mood and atmosphere of the time. Some have survived, others have not – among them, Jim Barratt, Nell Dowdall, Frank Chalcroft, Henry Sara, Stewart Purkis and Billy Williams.

My thanks to my wife, Daisy, to Hugo Dewar and Harry Wicks for helpful suggestions and useful references; to David Chalkley; and to Duncan Hallas for nudging me into the writing of these reminiscences.

Reg Groves August 1973

I

It is forty years since the anonymous publication of a duplicated journal, *The Communist*, made it known that an organized opposition existed inside the British Communist Party.

It called itself the British Section of the Left Opposition, a grand title for a group of less than a dozen people; and introduced itself in a front page article by saying:

> The Communist International is unable to gain the leadership of the world proletariat. It is – at this critical moment – unable, unready and unfit to lead the world revolution, and there is *no possible alternative*. The Left Opposition – led by Comrade Trotsky – is fighting to win back the CI to its task of leading the world revolution; the British group begins its work by the issue of this bulletin.[1]

Because of the heightening crisis in Germany, most of that first number was given over to Leon Trotsky's *Germany, the Key to the International Situation* which, written several months before, had since become even more pointed and relevant with its warning of looming disaster for the workers' movement in Germany, and ultimately in all Europe, unless Communist policies were changed in time.

That was in May 1932. At a specially summoned aggregate meeting of London CPers in July, accumulating criticism of the party leadership boiled over. The German question was one of several contentious issues raised, and there, in a conversation with Harry Pollitt, Stewart Purkis identified himself with Trotsky's views. On 27 July, Purkis wrote the letter to Pollitt: 'You have asked a straight question: you have a straight answer. You have asked me how far I go with *The Communist* . . . I go with it all the way'[2] – that was to bring, a few weeks later, his and Bill Williams' expulsion from the party.

Before they were thrown out, however, the party had acted against others, on matters not connected directly with *The Communist*. On 17 August Harry Wicks and Reg Groves[3] were expelled, Henry Sara 'suspended' and the Balham Group to which they belonged 'liquidated', accused of having 'held views fundamentally opposed to the policy of the Communist Party for some time past', and (unhappy formulation!) of having operated 'its own anti-working class line instead of that of the party'. Some of the members, the statement went on, supported by 'a majority in the Group, have deliberately engaged in anti-party factional activity in order to achieve this object. The leader of the Balham Group, R Groves, now openly declares his absolute opposition to the united front line of the party, particularly in connection with the World Anti-War Congress.'[4]

Members of the 'liquidated' group who desired 'to retain their membership of the party' were invited to a meeting 'for comradely discussion' with party officials on 19 August.[5] All but those expelled went along, but at this and other meetings and private interviews, the party functionaries were rebuffed. All wanted to stay in the party, but not at the price demanded – a stifling of discussion and a shuffling surrender to a leadership bent on the promotion of false policies.

The passing over of the Balham Group members,

together with Hugo Dewar of Tooting CP Group, gave the British Section a small but active membership in South-West London, and one with a base in the local working class movement. So long ago, so small an event, worth at most a line or two in the chronicles of our left movements – it is not surprising, then, that little has been written on it, or that what has, should have been either ill or inadequately informed. Some have seen it as prompted almost entirely by changes in Russian Communist and Communist International policies, by the onslaught between 1928 and 1932 on 'right deviationists' and 'conciliators', and by the Comintern's criticism of the British party leadership at the World Congress of 1928 and in a series of subsequent resolutions.[6] Others have seen it as the almost accidental outcome of inner-party discussions on trade union policy, with the expelled malcontents being driven into the Left Opposition; or as an outbreak of 'Left Sectarianism'; or as a pioneering episode in the story of British Trotskyism.

Segments of truth can be found in all these views. Our criticisms were inevitably couched in the formulae of Comintern resolutions and party textbooks; the Balham Group's policy challenges and earlier critical essays might easily have been smothered, and the group might have perished in the dark but for the Comintern's sustained attack upon the British party's leadership; and our own little contentions might have been washed away in the storm of official controversy, but for events in Spain and Germany in 1930–32 which together with the changes taking place in the British party, convinced us in the end that the disarray of the British party was no mere national peculiarity but endemic to the Comintern and its controller, the Russian party. True, we were woefully ignorant, particularly about the situation in Russia, and as we struggled for enlightenment and understanding and clarity, some of us found help in the writings of Trotsky and, to a lesser extent, in the periodicals published by the American Left Opposition.

All this conceded, there remains an unexplained residue – a group that went on to expulsion and ostracism, and to political ex-communication. To explain this it may help to say something about the people involved, and their relationships, to make some personal observations, and to start the story back in 1925. On 'Red Friday', on the eve of a lock-out of a million miners for rejecting lower pay and longer hours, rail and road transport unions placed on movements of coal an embargo that compelled hasty intervention by an unprepared Tory government. The government paid a subsidy to keep the pits open on the old terms until a Royal Commission had reported – giving the Tories time to make preparations for battle with the unions.

As the months passed, the conviction grew among socialists, trade unionists, labour folk, that only a general strike could prevent a renewal of the attack by government and employers on the miners, and then, on the rest of us.

It was soon after Red Friday that, at a crowded discussion meeting in John Groser's little back and front living rooms in Teviot Street, Poplar, I first met Stewart Purkis, Billy Williams and Bert Field, all three of them active in the Clearing House branch of the Railway Clerks' Association, the union's biggest, supposedly most reactionary branch, and active to such effect that, in May 1926, to the amazement of the union and the outraged indignation of the railway companies, a majority of branch members came out on strike in support of the miners, and held the line unbroken to the muddled, hopeless end of the strike.

Stewart: * forty, a socialist from 1904, an early en-

* Stewart Purkis, 1885–1969.

thusiast for Guild Socialism and various rebel causes, incisive, thorough in study and argument, bubbling with humour, yet in deadly earnest about the socialism which he lived as well as preached; Billy: * – in his mid-twenties, son of a Quaker-agnostic-building-worker-socialist-Welsh father, an omniverous reader, hard hitting in debate and in serious conversation, a good mixer but intolerant of the pompous, the slothful and the shoddy; and Bert Field: forty, affable, inarticulate, using his pipe to cover retreat from the more complicated controversies, and probably wiser than any of us. Such company, such mentors, and amid such stirring events, were exhilarating indeed to a raw but enthusiastic seventeen-year-old socialist like myself, and the friendships began then lasted for life.

As government preparations and intentions grew more pronounced, newspapers more abusive about the miners, and as Communist Party leaders were arrested and sent to prison, street meetings multiplied, arguments became more serious in the workshop; and in the trade union branch, we read, and talked after the meetings about events and books. One of the books was Trotsky's *Where is Britain Going?* published in 1925, an analysis of Britain's decline, and an argument on the need for political revolutions as a necessary preliminary to the social organisation of production and distribution, and of the certainty of capitalist resistance to such a revolution. At a time when open conflict between government and unions seemed certain, Trotsky's book had a considerable effect on us. We did not know, of course, that the book was, in Trotsky's own words, directed at the 'official conception' of the Comintern leadership with its hopes of 'an evolution to the left by the British General Council (TUC) and the pain-

* E S 'Billy' Williams, died 1963.

less penetration of Communism into the British Labour Party'. Nor did we suspect, then, that R Palme Dutt's defence of the book against labour and socialist critics was aimed also at the majority of the British Communist Party's leaders who saw the party as a militant wing of the reformist labour movement, not as an independent alternative to it.

We read also Trotsky's *The Lessons of October* (again unaware of controversies inside the Russian party, or that – as Harry Wicks has recently reminded us – there was some resistance among London communists to a blanket condemnation of the Russian oppositionists unheard). Trotsky's account of the role of Soviets and party in the insurrection, his demonstration that Bolshevism was not a theory but also 'a revolutionary system for teaching insurrection to the proletariat'; and his theme that 'The proletarian revolution cannot win if there is no party, or without the help of the party, or with a substitute for a party . . . The task of the Communist Party is to seize power and to transform society'[7] was argued over, but not yet accepted by us. There was much to find out about Marxism and the communism of Lenin, and some enlightening experiences to live through and observe before we came to see that a revolutionary party was needed.

The General Strike multiplied the arguments for such a party. Watching, with thousands of other workers, the convoys of food lorries and armoured cars rumbling out of the docks and along the Commercial Road; witnessing on the day of the TUC's abject surrender, brutal police attacks on a peaceful Poplar meeting and on scores of poor men's homes; the triumph displayed that day by our rulers and their toadies, and the ferocity of the employers' counter offensive – checked by a spontaneous rally of the strikers – it certainly seemed unlikely that the capitalists would allow power to pass from their hands without a struggle involving force. If so, a party of self-sacrificing, trained revolutionaries would be needed to prepare, guide and sustain the struggle for proletarian dictatorship – a Blanquist phrase coined when the proletariat was in a minority, but understood by us and most ordinary socialist and communist workers as meaning in contemporary conditions a government of the workers, a majority; and not, as it was to become in Russia, the dictatorship of a clique, ruling through a powerful bureaucracy.

The betrayal of the General Strike and the abandonment by the Labour leaders of the miners in the anguished months that followed, produced widespread disillusionment, slumped union membership, and a million and a half unemployed; the drop in wages, vengeful anti-union legislation by the Tory government drove the whole movement into the doldrums. Union leaders conferred with employers to secure 'rationalization' of industry – speed-up, more production by fewer workers, more unemployment – and an imposed industrial peace, with pay cuts and longer hours in the basic industries to make Britain's exports more 'competitive', until the capitalists of other lands did the same, and the whole process began all over again, a competition in becoming poorer and more wretched.

With all this, and having learned and studied and argued a way through to a conviction that the communists alone were trying to build a revolutionary party, Stewart Purkis, Billy Williams and I joined the party. Only the phlegmatic Bert Field remained outside, though he stayed a close friend and comrade, supporting Stewart Purkis and Billy Williams in union struggles, yet remaining a social democrat of the truest sort, a guild socialist, a militant, a sturdy witness to his beliefs. Curiously, in view of later events, soon after we joined, the party held a series of local members' meetings, addressed by party officials at which members were invited to approve the 'condemnation' of the Russian Left Opposition by the Russian Communist Party and Comintern. Some material by the Opposition was available, wedged in between massive corrective and condemnatory material; the issues involved included Russian economic policy, and the Comintern's policy in China. Purkis and Williams had pored hard and long over the Russian economic material, and at the St Pancras party meeting, unconvinced by the official case, abstained on this, or voted against. At the West London area meeting, I abstained on Russian economic policy and other matters, and voted against the official resolution on the Chinese question.

That no one rebuked us, or indeed showed any surprise or concern over our attitude would have been evidence to a Russian communist of the British party's backwardness. At this time, differences of opinion up to the deciding vote was what most party members took for granted, and most of us assumed that it was so in Russia. Before long, such doubts and abstentions let alone votes against, would become vilest heresy, bring expulsion, denunciation, victimisation – and in Russia imprisonment and execution.

Things were far from well in the British party. Membership, which had doubled during 1926, had halved in 1927. Sales of party periodicals and pamphlets fell, and went on falling. Policy was still directed at hopeful reform of the official movement, and the party still called for 'all power to the TUC General Council', the selfsame General Council that had surrendered abjectly in May 1926 and that had abandoned the miners in the long lockout that had followed.

Despite rebuffs, the party sought affiliation to the Labour Party, which was expelling communists from individual membership, beginning to bar them as delegates from trade unions to constituency Labour Party management committees and national conferences, and expelling any local parties that refused to expel or bar communists. Some twenty-four of these parties or sections of parties, had, by 1927, been organized in the National Left Wing Movement, a confusing masquerade which led to many communists giving time and energy needed by their own party to sustain the 'original' local Labour Party in elections and other activities against the more recently established 'official Labour Party'. The National Left Wing Movement was, like so many of the auxiliaries, a substitute for the party, not an extension of it.

The party was still calling for 'a Labour government', adding such phrases as 'but make it fight'; or demanding, as did the 7th Plenum of the Comintern (ECCI), a 'real Labour government'.[8] Even as late as January 1928, the adroit, plausible, wily Andrew Rothstein, who may have already received hints of sharp changes in Russian and Comintern policy when the fateful 9th Plenum was assembling, was too deeply embedded in the routine of office and the old policy to grasp the full import of what was happening. He could be found calling on the one hand for 'a sharpening of the fight against reformism' and on the other for 'a real change of leadership' in the Labour Party. He urged the National Left Wing Movement to replace a score or so reformist parliamentary candidates by 'honest revolutionary fighters', members of the Labour Party of course, who would run as Labour candidates in the elections'.[9] The decisions of the 9th Plenum were 'unanimously endorsed' by the British party's Political Bureau and Central Committee. 'The 9th Plenum' said Tom Bell, in that convoluted phraseology which owed as much to his being a Scot as to the perils of political life in the Comintern, 'drew attention to the tendency towards a definite merging of the trade union organizations and the labour bureaucracy with the State apparatus . . . It was necessary for the party to adopt a sharper tactic towards the Labour Party and the trade union leaders. This was the tactic of "class against class".'[10]

According to Bell, the party's 10th Congress at Bermondsey in January 1929, 'unreservedly adopted the new line'. But Bell was not only a party elder, and so one of those very much responsible for the 'old line', he was also – as the British party's representative at the Comintern – visiting other national sections, chiding them as 'right deviationists', that is, as followers of that very same 'old line'. He was also, according to Allen Hutt, 'Among the majority of those who were then the principal party leaders, men who had come over from the previously existing Socialist groupings and bore strong marks of sectarian dogmatism in their outlook', who showed 'a strange hesitancy in appreciating the need for the party now to assert its full independence and to change its tactics and approach accordingly'.

'And so', Hutt goes on, 'from the end of 1927 there was waged for two years the keenest battle of ideas the party had so far known around the question of its "new line". This new line sought to prescribe a new independence for the Communist Party both in political and economic struggles . . . it represented a necessary break with the past. As such it was stubbornly resisted by the dominant section of the party leadership . . . Thorough-going changes in the leadership were obviously necessary if the party was not to stagnate. These were not finally achieved till the party's congress held at Leeds in December, 1929.'[11]

As will be seen, the necessary changes were not achieved at Leeds; but Hutt, a lively and able critic, was one of the dozen or so potential candidates for party leadership invited to Moscow for a year's course at the Lenin School. I was the only one who refused to go, believing that the struggle in the British party was far from ended. As with most of those who went, Hutt's critical faculty atrophied rapidly, and he was to serve the Stalinized party faithfully through all the policy changes, through all the Stalin-worship, party purges, imprisonments, trials and executions. His account omits much, particularly the extent to which the Comintern dictated the terms of discussion and outcome, but it does not exaggerate the discontent among the members in 1929.

It was early in 1929 that Henry Sara* first became associated with the three of us and with others in our circle, which included my wife Daisy, Steve Dowdall, a tiler-bricklayer and founder member of the party, his wife Nell, and her sister Daisy, both of the Tailor and Garment Workers' Union, and active members of the party since mid-1926.

Living in North London, Henry Sara soon became, like myself, a frequent caller at the Express Dairy teashop close to Euston station, where Stewart and Billy lunched each day on bread, cheese and coffee, and where books, politics and party affairs were talked about, often irreverently and sometimes hilariously. Henry, tall, strong of build, with eloquent, resonant voice, and a commanding platform manner, incisive, informed in debate and discussion, brought much to us in the way of knowledge of Marxism, socialist theory and labour history. His critical faculty had been toughened by early associations with

* Henry Sara, 1886–1953.

anarchist ideas and the stricter industrial unionism groups; by his experiences during the 1914–18 war, when after a courageous anti-militarist campaign of public meetings he was arrested and conscripted into the army. He refused to obey orders or wear a uniform, was maltreated and finally sent to prison. A popular outdoor orator in Finsbury Park and elsewhere before, during and after the war, and a skilful lecturer at socialist and secularist halls all over the country, he had hesitated to join the Communist Party at the time of its foundation, knowing as he did most of its leading personalities from pre-war days. But a visit to Russia, where the revolution was still in rags and struggling to survive, decided him, though the suppression of the Kronstadt uprising caused him some uneasiness, and was perhaps one reason why he avoided being drawn into the inner circles of the party leadership.

By now, Stewart Purkis and I were on the London District Committee, and for most of 1929 I was its assistant-organizer. The London District Committee office adjoined that of the almost non-existent Young Communist League, from which William Rust, who had assumed the role of Comintern spokesman, aided by the more likeable Walter Tapsell, conducted a campaign against the old leadership and for his own elevation to power.

As the General Election of 1929 approached, the party leadership, committed to the slogans of 'Class Against Class' and 'A Revolutionary Workers' Government', was again shaken by controversy. In March five members of the Central Committee voted that where no Communist candidates were running, the workers should be advised to vote Labour. In the election, twenty-five party candidates polled 50,644 votes, most of them faring miserably. Only in a few constituencies did the vote reach four figures. Labour, with over eight million voters and

288 seats, took office, with Ramsay MacDonald as Prime Minister.

A whole series of factors re-stimulated criticism of the leadership: the scanty vote, a membership fall from 10,000 in 1926 to some 3,500 in 1929, periodicals kept alive and functionaries paid only by Comintern subsidies; a diminished but devoted band of members who by sheer persistence and by appearing in many places, on many occasions, under many titles and banners, alone made the party seem larger and more important than it was. There were demands for a special conference. The attack on the resolution drawn up by the Central Committee, was led by the London, Tyneside and – to a lesser extent – Manchester, District Committees. The Tynesiders, led by Maurice Ferguson, were rabidly 'Comintern line' men;[12] the London District was less so, though its resolution, compiled at long and wearying committee meetings, often prodded into angry argument by interjections, expostulations and tirades from attending representatives of the Political Bureau, tended to keep to accepted phrases and formulations. The London resolution, indeed, showed a marked independence of approach over a matter on which the Comintern and Russian leaders were most sensitive. The Central Committee resolution said, 'We completely endorse the measures that have been taken by the ECCI (Comintern) in the struggles against the Right Wingers and the Conciliators in its own ranks and in the parties . . .' London District Committee dissented, saying, 'This presupposes that the party as a whole has a fair knowledge of the inner-party situations of these sections. This information the party has not got and for the party to understand this statement it must have in its possession more complete information'. London's resolution was approved at an aggregate meeting of London members, at which

Rothstein and 'Jock' Wilson, strident and politically un-couth, angered the membership by their abuse of the district committee and by a blatantly dishonest defence of the majority party leadership.[13]

The 10th Plenum of the ECCI condemned the British party leadership in language that was to become depress-ingly familiar in subsequent years. It called on the party to 'intensify the fight against Social Democracy, which is the chief support of capitalism', to wage 'an energetic struggle against the "left" wing of Social Democracy', to 'eradicate from its (own) ranks all remnants of Right opportunist deviations'. Noting that 'conciliation, which appeared as cowardly opportunism, screening avowed liquidationism, has recently slipped over to the Right Wing position . . .', the Plenum demanded 'that the conciliators openly and emphatically disassociate themselves from the Right de-viators, conduct an active fight . . . against the Right devi-ation . . . *Submit implicitly to all decisions of the Comintern and its sections, and actively carry them out. Failure will place the culprits outside the ranks of the Communist International.*'[14]

Reading this uneasily, we saw the Central Committee, including those so splenetic against London and other critical Districts, 'endorse' Comintern decisions and com-mands, and 'welcome'(!) the critical resolutions of London, Newcastle and Manchester, saying, 'The party member-ship has been in advance of the leadership in appreciating the new situation and desiring the more energetic carry-ing through of the new line.[15] We watched critics and criti-cised alike scurrying to obey and conform to the latest commands, and leading Central Committee members twist-ing themselves into most abject postures to placate the Comintern and retain their posts. We grew less and less sure in our minds that the Comintern's extending control and direction of policy and people was a good thing.

But, on the hopeful side, was the critical, determined mood of the members, the possibility that a new leadership would emerge from the discussion, and from the coming party congress. Britain's first communist daily paper, the *Daily Worker*, was promised for 1 January 1930. Discontent with the Labour government which was retreating from even modest plans to reduce unemployment, was growing among the workers. And, though bankers, economists and politicians dispensed optimistic forecasts for the coming year, already there were cracks on the surface of optimism and complacency. The first signs were detectable of what was to be world capitalism's most serious economic crisis.

For the third time in a decade, a potentially revolutionary situation was on its way. Would there this time be a truly revolutionary party to keep the rendezvous?

On the eve of the party congress, R Palme Dutt wrote, privately, of the congress:

> The supreme need is that the positive lead from all contributing must be strong. It is necessary to start one's thinking out of the present position of the party in the working class, of the line of advance of the party, of the consequent *role of the Congress* in the total political situation and in the historical development of the British working class . . .
>
> The primary problem and task for us in relation to the economic struggle is, first, to fight the way forward for the independent action of the masses, and lead it, and second, to *develop the political character of the gathering economic* struggles, to develop the consciousness of the masses through them for further struggle and advance to a new plane.[16]

Perhaps, after all, out of bitter argument and controversy, would come a renewal of revolutionary purpose and the first useful steps to the creation of that party to which all of us were committed.

So – it was heigh-ho for Leeds, and that special congress, where, if all went well, faded reformist policies would be replaced by bright new revolutionary ones, and where old leaders were to be put down, and new ones raised up.

2

Expectation was high among delegates assembled on 30 November 1929, at Leeds, for the CPGB's eleventh congress. And when they departed three days later, the mood was hopeful among most. Under sustained attack, led by the district committee members of London, Newcastle and Manchester, the new policies appeared to have been adopted fully. Many of the leaders most associated with the 'old line' had been removed from positions of importance – only twelve of the old Central Committee remained, and twenty-three new ones had been added.[17]

Yet it was a dusty triumph. Noisy and passionate debates took place in the hall, but the real decisions were made behind the scenes. The new leadership was chosen from above, not elected from below. A 'recommended' panel was substituted for normally elected members; there were to be no more 'social-democratic methods of election'; the new Central Committee members were chosen 'for practical reasons, and their understanding of the present period, their experience in the conduct of class battles, and their capacity for carrying out the political tasks of the party', making possible *the more energetic fulfilment of the obligations that are imposed on our party as a section of the Communist International*,[18] or, as Wally Tapsell put it more succinctly, a leadership which would strive to carry out the line of the Comintern'.[19]

Personal recollections of the congress have been

blurred by time, and its documents tell little. Re-read, they bring only a weariness of spirit, an incredulity that these dry papers, containing only falsehoods and false-seeming, empty of disinterested argument, creative thought and humanity, could have been taken seriously by so many bright and brave souls among the small and mostly dedicated membership.

A few vivid impressions remain of the congress itself – a recollection of Wal Hannington and Arthur Horner, the party's only genuine mass leaders, in the shadows as being of the right, yet vigorous and defiant in explanation of their views; a perspiring, brow-mopping Bob Lovell, of the almost non-existent British section of the International Class War Prisoners' Aid, making vituperative attacks on the left, as he defended the lurid stunts and provocative clashes with the police by which he secured newspaper headlines and approval and continued support from his Moscow employers.

Distinct, too, is recollection of the resentful abasement of some of the 'old line' leaders as they strove to hold their places by abject and dishonourable 'confession'; of Harry Pollitt, acknowledged leader of the party, being allowed to state his case for postponement of *Daily Worker* publication to 1 May, – without oratorial embellishments lest he carry the delegates with him – and then, afterwards, dutifully 'confessing' his error in having advocated such a proposition; of knots of animated delegates arguing in the corridors; of Pollitt taking Stewart Purkis aside and attempting to coax him into tempering his opposition, and Stewart, unruffled and courteous, refusing.

And, distinct in the memory, yet puzzling, the strange little meeting almost conspiratorially arranged, between some London delegates, and the Comintern representative, Walter Ulbricht of Germany.

We stood at one end of the room, the impassive, aloof Ulbricht at the other. Presently, we were beckoned before the presence. Ulbricht spoke in German, an interpreter passed his words on to us. We learned with surprise that all the great man wanted was an assurance that London members' objections to Johnny Campbell remaining in commanding party positions were political objections not personal ones. It was left to Stewart Purkis to reply for us, and he assured the interpreter that we all had the greatest respect and affection for Campbell, but felt that he was too deeply embedded in the old ways and policies to perform adequately where the new policies were concerned. The interpreter, baffled by the amiability shown and the jargon-free vocabulary, juggled the words in the air for a moment before passing them to Ulbricht in more formal terms. The great man nodded at us, and faded from the scene. The interview was over.

We were uneasy about the way things had gone at Leeds, but reluctant to examine the full implications. Chiefly, we shied away from the matter of growing Russian party control over the international movement, and from attempting to estimate what might be happening in Russia itself. We told ourselves that Russia, a backward country, devastated by war, civil war and wars of intervention, hampered by blockade and capitalist hostility, was now engaged in a gigantic programme of industrialization. Some measure of dictatorship was still required. Faults of omission and commission were due to these circumstances. Adverse reports on conditions in Russia came almost entirely from malignant and blatantly untruthful capitalist-owned newspapers and politicians, the enemies of revolution, socialism and the working peoples. How could we then give credence to criticisms of Russia?

Pushing aside our uncertainties, we threw ourselves into our party activities. In struggle and action differences would be resolved, errors on all our parts corrected, experience and understanding enlarged.

The *Daily Worker* duly appeared on 1 January 1930, edited by William Rust, in itself a guarantee that it would be drab and colourless, and inhibited from experiment and adventure by fear of deviation. A series of wholesalers' boycotts put a considerable burden on the small, overworked membership, who in many places had to meet late-night or early-morning trains, collect and distribute to local newsagents bundles of the paper. A declaration of war on 'capitalist sport' by the Comintern compelled the dropping of football, cricket and racing reports and 'tips'; and as most workers could afford but one daily newspaper, down came the already sadly drooping sales.

When editorial board and party leadership inclined to blame the members for the falling sales, there were exasperated protests. Some came from members of the Battersea local; and these discussions, and talks between Stewart Purkis, Billy Williams and myself, led to a letter of some length being sent by me to the party secretariat on 26 February, discussing the role of a daily paper in the workers' struggle, and suggesting among other things reporting in depth of major or unusually important industrial conflicts, bringing background, industry and the people involved to life for the workers everywhere.[20] These and other suggestions were ignored or brushed aside.

Yet, by June 1930, Rust himself was complaining:

'The whole party must face the fact that just as the party membership is small and stagnant, so is the circulation of the *Daily Worker* very low and unsatisfactory. The basic reason for the still unsatisfactory party situation is the mistakes of the leadership, which failed to mobilize the membership for a systematic and daily struggle against opportunism.'

The *Daily Worker* should be used for a 'ruthless war against opportunism in practice, against right-wing passivity and left sectarianism. . . .'[21] So the *Daily Worker* was not primarily a paper for working people but an instrument for imposing Moscow-directed policies on the British party!

In early March I offered to write voluntarily a column called *A Worker's Notebook*, over the pseudonym 'Plowman' and the offer was accepted.[22] I wrote it every day, helped out only by an occasional paragraph from Stewart Purkis, and took it each morning from South-West London to Tabernacle Street, using a sixpenny all-day tram ticket. The column went its troubled way until 30 May when, because of continual editorial suppression and alteration, I quit. Though most of the political differences that flared up were argued out in correspondence,[23] the curious will find in published material some evidence of the differences that arose.[24]

Two paragraphs in the *Notebook* may be noted as indicative of our critical views at the time. One referred to an article by Bukharin that compared, with superb irony undetected by the party leaders, the disciplines of Jesuit and Communist. In commending the article to *Daily Worker* readers, the *Notebook* quoted a passage describing the Jesuit theory of subordination:

'Every member of the order must submit to his superior, "like a corpse which can be turned in any direction; like a stick which submits to every movement; like a lump of wax which can be made to change its shape and to stretch in any direction".'[25]

That we saw in this an illusion to the discipline being imposed on Russian party and Comintern sections, suggests that our eyes were being opened to the real situation of the revolutionary movement.

Nearer home, and of more immediate concern to us, was another item commended in the *Notebook* – Freda Utley's review of the two volumes of Lenin's works, *The Iskra Period*. Freda, whom we first met and became friendly with when she fought Westminster as a Communist candidate in the 1928 London County Council elections, drew attention to Lenin's attacks on the 'economists' – described by him as those that 'bow down before spontaneity, gaze with awe upon the posteriors of the Russian proletariat, and think it sufficient in the party press merely to reflect the drab day to day struggle, so that the workers read the paper once or twice and then say "awfully dull".' Freda went on, 'who can deny that 'economism' is strong in our ranks? . . . But, comrades, it is not enough to repeat the slogans 'Down with the social-fascist Labour Government' and 'A revolutionary workers' government', and feel that in so doing you have fulfilled the task of raising the political consciousness of the workers.'[26]

Freda Utley's world-wide researches into the textile industry had led to her concern over party propaganda and activities among the Lancashire cotton workers. Local and industry-wide resistance to reorganization, speed-up, lower pay and mass unemployment was necessary – but was it not the party's duty to make plain to the workers that the outdated British capitalist textile industry, facing growing competition from the cheap-labour, highly modernized textile industries of the East, would be driven inexorably to continuous reductions in pay and employment? And that the workers had to choose between going along with the employers in this desperate and ultimately ineffectual course to 'keep the industry competitive', or of taking the way of resistance to worsening conditions – socialist revolution, socialist internationalism and social ownership?[27]

To communists it was axiomatic that in Britain's older and major industries, capitalism could survive only by the lowering of living standards at home and the exploitation of colonial peoples and resources abroad. Stewart Purkis did for the railways what Freda Utley had done for textiles, and analyzed the situation and prospects for the railway workers under capitalism. The railway companies' decline was a crisis of capitalism, and '*inside capitalism, all industries will increasingly prove unable to maintain both wages and profits. . . . That every railwayman may master this basic fact should be the main political concern of the revolutionary who participates in the railway struggle.*'[28] The party's political bureau denounced Utley and Purkis for 'attacking the leadership that has a correct political line and is also paying considerable attention to improving the understanding of the whole party.'[29] If the critical formulations here were not completely adequate, arising as they did from examinations of particular industries, yet the issue underlying the argument was a vital one, for it concerned the reciprocal relations between the battles of the hour and the revolutionary uprising which was the party's supposed aim, indeed, the reason for its existence. How far we were as a party from understanding this reciprocity was shown during the dispute in the woollen industry in 1930.

Here were assembled all the essential elements in the revolutionary argument – a declining major industry, already afflicted by falling wages and employment; employers pressing for further wage reductions; a vigorous rejection of the cuts by the workers; and intervention in the dispute by the Labour government, which took the form of a supposedly impartial inquiry and which inevitably reported in favour of wage reductions. Despite faintheartedness on the part of officials of some of the unions involved, the workers voted down the recommended cuts, and were locked out.

Sent by the party to the West Riding for a week of outdoor meetings; walking the lamplit, cobbled streets of Dewsbury and Batley; watching the trams climbing the streets between rows and rows of little stone houses, gaunt silent mills and forests of smokeless chimneys; listening to the talk of locked-out men and women, and of the older men whose fathers or grandfathers had been Chartists, or radicals and socialists of the early days, it was impossible not to be reminded again of what the *Daily Worker* could have been – what might have been done here, in the lockout, given the character and quality of the people, their long traditions of struggle. Riches indeed with which to give life and colour to the presentation of the revolutionary cause.

As it was, the *Daily Worker* sloganized this struggle as it sloganized all struggles, large or small, making it faceless and drab. To anyone on the spot, the slogans appeared to have nothing whatever to do with the course of events, nor did they seem to have any meaning for those directly engaged in the battle. In the Bradford area the party's main work, except for a parade of outdoor meetings, was the distribution of relief to locked-out men and women in need. This was organized by Isobel Brown, on behalf of the Moscow-controlled and financed Workers' International Relief, one of the many party front organizations. A non-representative, nebulous 'action committee' met in the building, and there also Ernie Brown, Isobel's husband, addressed the workers who came to the centre. The political content of his speeches was obscure – his speciality seemed to be 'cheerin' t'lads oop', with a comedy style reminiscent of his native Lancashire. It was obvious that the party had no influence on the course or outcome of the battle, nor was it attracting to its ranks the more thoughtful workers.

Returning to London when the week ended, I reported to Harry Pollitt. He said nothing, asked me for a written report, and handed me a week's pay, which I refused. Nothing came of the written report; and, after several weeks of unbroken solidarity, the unions decided to negotiate separate settlements and the workers returned to work. At a West Riding by-election held soon afterwards, the Labour vote fell drastically, the Tory was elected, and a Communist candidate polled 700 votes.

So brief a chronicle as this, compressing events as it must, necessarily emphasizes disproportionately our opposition to the party's leadership, as though this occupied all our waking thoughts and actions. It didn't. Our time was taken almost exclusively by our party work – the frequent parades and gatherings under a variety of banners; the sale of party papers; union branch, party group, committee and fraction meetings; as well as, for some, a deal of speaking, lecturing and writing. Opposition to aspects of party policies grew out of our party work and experience, and was intended as a contribution to the discussion and formulation of policy. We were not an organized group but close friends who talked things over, and who individually expressed our views openly to our party comrades.

Stewart Purkis, expelled from his union in 1929 for his party activities, but still strongly supported and re-

B

spected by his fellow workers, edited, with Billy Williams, a lively cyclostyled paper, *The Jogger*; and, in collaboration with some Idris workers at the Camden Town factory, the *Idris Ginger* which, with its vigorous presentation of the workers' grievances and its brief, simple exposition in each number of Marxian economics and communist policy, came to be regarded as a model of what a factory paper should be. Both Purkis and Williams were active in the St Pancras local, on various London District Committee sub-committees, and busy among railway militants in the NUR and ASLEF.

Steve and Nell Dowdall, and my wife Daisy and I, were active in the South-West London local, busy in various Battersea groups, finally being settled in the Nine Elms rail group, and responsible for the sale at the rail depot of the cyclostyled *Nine Elms Signal*, though almost all of us lived in Balham, and no one in the group worked on the railways, much less at Nine Elms.

It was towards the end of 1930 that Harry Wicks first became associated with us, having returned in August to his native Battersea, after three years at the Lenin School in Moscow. As a lad working on the railway, Harry had joined the Daily Herald League, which in 1921 went over almost entirely to the newly-founded Communist Party. Harry went with it, helped to form a Young Communist League (YCL) in Battersea; and took part in the production and distribution of the Nine Elms *Spark* and the Victoria *Signal* up to the time of the General Strike. Elected to the YCL executive in 1926, in the following year he was selected to be sent to the Latin School. Harry brought us much – he had witnessed episodes in the struggle in the Comintern and the Russian party between the increasingly powerful Stalin group and the Left Opposition, he knew of many international controversies and personalities – and he also knew Battersea, its radical traditions, and its active socialist and Communist Party workers. Harry Wicks was to join us as we renewed our criticisms of the leadership early in the year 1931.

Busy indeed was the life in those times of the Communist Party member, and we were as busy as any. But there were occasional summer afternoons at cricket, and some Saturday or Friday nights when we walked through the crowded New Cut market with its stalls, its loquacious stallholders and its roaring naphthalene flares, to the Waterloo Road and the Old Vic, queued and paid five pence and climbed the stairs to the gallery; and saw our Shakespeare staged by Harcourt Williams and spoken by a superb company closer to the original text, pace and style than any before or since. And as we came out under the stars, into the rain-washed streets, odd words sometimes lingered in the mind as strangely apt to our party activities. Like the sharp exchange from the first part of Henry IV, when Owen Glendower says:

"I can call spirits from the vasty deep"

and Hotspur retorts:

"Why, so can I, or so can any man:
But will they come when you do call them?"

Would they come, indeed? During 1930, the party leadership produced yet another 'front' organization behind which and in which the party could attempt – vainly – to hide itself and its political identity. This was the campaign for the 'Workers' Charter' – the name was based on the People's Charter of 1837. The Workers' Charter began with six points, immediate demands for those at work and those unemployed: the demands grew to nine, then to fifteen points, but when, after nearly a year's activity, a monster conference was held at Bermondsey on 12 April 1931, of the 316 organizations represented there, only sixty-eight union branches and seven co-op guilds could be called genuine, non-party organizations.[30]

The ballyhoo lasted a few more weeks; the spirits refused to come from the vasty deep or from anywhere else. By June, William Rust was writing: 'United front work is practically non-existent, as is shown by the weakness of the Charter campaign: our slogans are far too general, and the Minority Movement tends to be a duplicate of the party. We have not yet succeeded in organizing the daily fight in a revolutionary manner; our revolutionary policy for the way out of the capitalist crisis remains abstract, and is mechanically presented.'[31]

R P Dutt, too, found the Charter campaign unsatisfactory – it was liable to be 'misunderstood as some kind of all-round programme of reforms, a kind of minimum programme to meet the crisis.' This was not so. 'The Charter cannot solve the crisis. . . . The Charter is not a programme in the sense of a programme of a party . . . but simply "common ground" on the most immediate issues of the class struggle.' But, went on Dutt, members, while fighting for these issues alongside non-party workers, should 'spread the understanding of the revolutionary line of Communism which can alone conquer the crisis and bring final victory.'[32]

Unfortunately, the freedom of thought and action required by a revolutionary party to change its points of emphasis and adapt to swiftly-moving events no longer existed. Initiative had been destroyed, improvization inhibited. Those attempting to stimulate discussion on the necessary reciprocity between immediate battles and the revolutionary uprising, between objective and subjective factors, had been denounced and silenced. Even Rust and Dutt had not confessed until a dissatisfied Comintern had demanded that the British party should produce results commensurate with the objective situation.

The party members could but go on as before. The programmes of immediate demands designed to deceive workers into an unsuspecting support of the party, deceived only the party membership. Such attempted deceptions and the continual and indiscriminate abuse of the 'social-fascists' of all ranks and opinions – an obligatory act if Comintern approval was to be ensured – made many socialist workers suspicious of the party; and the excessive attacks on the 'left' as the biggest political scoundrels of all made the situation worse. An assured, firmly-held independent view would have enabled a flexibility of tactics and relationships to be possible, and in a rapidly changing situation, such flexibility, allied to a firm revolutionary position, was vital if the party was to influence events. But the revolutionary certainty was not there – only the 'immediate demands'.

For the economic storm blowing across the entire capitalist world was becoming a mighty tempest. By January 1931, out of an insured working population of 12.4 million Britain had 2,662,824 registered as unemployed. Many hundreds of thousands outside insurance were unemployed but unregistered, or working but part-time. Nearly a million were on poor relief.

As the numbers of unemployed rose, the Labour government, which had long abandoned its modest election programme of reforms, and which had almost angrily rejected plans to provide employment, now turned to the orthodox capitalist remedies for slump – massive economies in public spending at the expense of the social services; cuts in pay in public and private industries and services; drastic cuts in unemployment benefit, in the period of benefit and in eligibility for benefit.

Throughout the cheap compromises, and now through the period of 'tough measures', the large majority of Labour MPs supported the government, and turned savagely on the tiny group of Independent Labour Party (ILP) members in the Commons who spoke and voted against the government's broken promises and failure to act on behalf of the unemployed. When the Mosley plan for providing work was rejected by the cabinet, the Labour MPS also voted the plan down by 202 votes to 29, and went on backing MacDonald, Snowden, Thomas, Henderson and the rest. When the Labour cabinet appointed, in February 1931, an 'economies' commission headed by Sir George May of the Prudential, only a score of Labour MPS voted against it, the rest voting for it; and Snowden's April budget, which pointed the conditions for subsequent economies, received also the support of most Labour MPS.

The May committee reported, recommending massive economies in social services and other state expenditure; cuts in the pay of teachers, the armed forces and civil servants; and a reduction in unemployment benefit of 20 per cent. The Labour cabinet went along with two-thirds of the proposed cuts, was considering, and might well have agreed to, almost all of the rest, when there was an angry intervention by the general council of the TUC, expressing adamant opposition to nearly all the 'economies'.[33] Even then, when a cabinet vote was taken on the one issue made crucial and decisive as a condition of support by British, French and American bankers, and by the leaders of the Liberal and Conservative Parties in the Commons, that of the cut in unemployment benefit, twelve cabinet ministers voted for the cut, and only eight voted against.

Prime Minister MacDonald went to Buckingham Palace to resign – or, at least, that was the story. Next day he met his Labour colleagues to dismiss them, and explain that he was now head of an 'emergency' government, a coalition completely dependent upon Liberal and Conservative votes. Only Chancellor Philip Snowden, Lord Privy Seal, J H Thomas, and a handful of junior ministers, went with him. The Labour Party was now the opposition, but an opposition rendered ineffectual and completely discredited by Labour's behaviour and record when in government, by its sponsorship and acceptance of the 'cuts', and of the orthodox capitalist economics from which they were derived – the economics of enforced scarcity in a world of plenty.

For the massive retrenchment espoused by Labour as well as by the parties of capital, took place in a world where, for several years, output of food, raw materials and manufactures had risen steeply, far outstripping the growth of population. There was enough and to spare to feed, clothe and house the working millions of the world. But the remedy applied by the capitalist financiers, industrialists and politicians was the deliberate restoration of scarcity by closing the mills, mines and factories, cutting the wages of those still at work, destroying all kinds of crops including foodstuffs, letting land go out of cultivation, and limiting drastically the production of raw materials. The bread lines stretched across the world. One hundred million were estimated to be unemployed. In Britain, by the autumn of 1931, the registered unemployed totalled 2,824,774, and a million were on poor relief. The crisis of capitalism was plain for all to see. That its overthrow alone could provide reasonable provision for the people could now be plainly demonstrated. Objectively, for the third time since the war, the elements of a potential revolutionary situation were discernible.

On 25 August, the *Daily Worker* published the party's pronouncement on the crisis. Its content called for immediate protest; but a hurried letter from myself, published next day in the *Worker*, and two subsequent letters which were not published – 'the opening of a party discussion at the present moment is no way desirable' wrote the political bureau – were inadequate, and in some ways over-cautious in formulation, mainly through anxiety to give the party leadership no pretext to exaggerate minor issues into monstrous heresies (a method learned from Comintern and Russian party leaders) so blotting out the major arguments. As it was, one or two bogies were raised which were to haunt us for a long time to come; and it is possible that we would have done better to have spoken out, irrespective of possible misrepresentation.[34]

As we came to see it, in those last August weeks and early September, the party's forces were small, isolated from the main body of workers, unprepared, and immersed in operations and agitations unrelated to the development of the crisis. We communists were far too few to determine by ourselves the way things went. But there were leaders of the workers everywhere, active in factories, mills, union branches, trades councils, socialist societies and even Labour parties, hostile to capitalism and the employers, awake now, or partly so, to the ominous attacks on standards of living, prepared to resist and, maybe, in the course of the struggle, to go all the way with the revolution.

These local and industrial leaders would be to the fore, in the front line of the workers' resistance to the cuts. Here could be mobilized a multitude of militants, close to the people and toughened politically by recent events.

Somehow in each area a centre of struggle had to be created around which the workers could unite, debate and decide each step of the struggle. In many areas, the trades councils might provide this leadership and centre, but many of them had been reduced in strength, had expelled communists, and, as a consequence of the 1927 anti-trade union act, had divided themselves into separate political and industrial bodies. In such cases, improvised organization might be needed – committees or councils of action.

What we did in South-West London – where our group numbered less than a dozen, and where the whole party membership in Battersea and Wandsworth amounted to no more than a few dozen, was to make contact with the active militants and socialists in our area. In the first few days of September, one or two of us visited the ILP branches at Tooting and Clapham. Both branches were affiliated, as were all ILP branches, to the local Labour parties in the two constituencies; both had supported the small group of ILP members in the Commons who had defied Labour Party rules to speak and vote against the government's treatment of the unemployed, and so had clashed with local Labour Party mandarins. We went to them honestly, saying in effect that though we held to our revolutionary views and would go on advocating them, and expected them to stick to their opinions, too, we thought we could work together to unite workers' resistance to the cuts and for a socialist answer to the crisis. They responded generously, particularly in Clapham, and together we began to recruit from union branches, co-operative guilds and Labour Party wards, members for our committee, which was soon in regular session at the New Morris Hall in Clapham. In mid-September we threw a line of outdoor meetings across south-west London, covering Brixton, Clapham, Battersea and Tooting, and these we maintained at regular intervals throughout September and October.

Parliament assembled in September. The communist-led National Unemployed Workers' Movement (NUWM) and other organizations called on the unemployed to demonstrate outside Parliament; crowds came, not only the stalwarts of the NUWM from every London borough, but thousands of others, anonymous, bewildered, indignant, shaken out of quietude by the raging storm of economic crisis, and now drawn together in protest.

> *We are fellows still,*
> *Serving alike in sorrow:*
> *Leak'd is our bark,*
> *And we poor mates,*
> *Stand on the dying deck,*
> *Hearing the surge's threat . . .*

As darkness fell, the crowd grew, stretching away under the street lights as far as the eye could see. In front of Parliament, the mounted police charged again and again at the swirling crowds of cloth-capped men . . .

A tense excitement not felt since the General Strike was noticeable at all the local indoor and outdoor meetings. Where there were usually scores, there now were hundreds, and on occasions a thousand or more. The upturned, lamplit faces were serious, anxious, hopeful that the apostles of change, of class struggle, of revolution, would tell them what to do. Excitement grew when, on 15 September, the men of the Atlantic Fleet at Invergordon refused to obey orders to sail, and, in tidy Navy fashion, took over the ships, 'refusing to serve under the new rates of pay'. The government quickly appeased the sailors; but teachers and civil servants, not given in that period to militant protest, now marched and met in great numbers. In Britain's major cities, the unemployed in tens and scores of thousands surged in turbulent protest, often clashing violently with the police. The men of money began shifting their cash away from Britain, government credit tumbled and on 20 September, a government set up to keep Britain on the gold standard was forced to go off it. On 11 October postal workers, civil servants, teachers, unemployed and trade unionists staged a 100,000-strong united demonstration in Hyde Park.

Somewhere during those first few weeks of the crisis, the balance of forces shifted, the mood of the people changed subtly, imperceptibly, and the revolutionary prospect receded – though the battle against the cuts went on, and, it should be emphasized, went on under the leadership of the local militants all over the country. But without clearly communicated aims and a related strategy of progressively extending struggle, the militants in workshop, union branch and at labour exchange had nothing in the way of political ideas and purposes around which to rally and unite the movement – except resistance to the cuts. No visible, acceptable alternative emerged to the hopelessly compromised and discredited Labour Party leadership, which foundered and faltered still more in the swiftly-snatched election of 16 to 27 October, described by the *Manchester Guardian* as the 'shortest, strangest and most fraudulent of our time'. The combined Liberal and Conservative vote gave the 'National' government an overwhelming electoral victory and inflicted a crushing defeat on the Labour Party, which held only fifty-two seats, approximately its representation in 1910. Only our failure as communists to create – under fire – a revolutionary party allowed the Labour Party subsequently to restore its influence over the workers.

In the election, 26 CPGB candidates polled 72,824 votes; and 43,892 of these were polled in four constituencies where conditions were especially favourable. The Central Committee admitted: 'In many cases the difference in principle between the policy of the CP and the policy of the reformists was not at all made clear in the election campaign . . . The party has absolutely failed to express the revolutionary way out of the crisis in concrete terms that the masses can understand . . .'

In South-West London, our committee, or council of action as we had named it (hopefully but, I think, wrongly) was expanding and recruiting support in local union branches, at regular outdoor meetings, and at the labour exchanges, where we now led the local unemployed organization. The group had become the 'Balham Group', and had been strengthened by the transfer to it of Jim Barrett, a party member of nine years standing; and by the recruiting of some younger people, Cyril Whiting, Maurice Simmonds, Bill Pyne and Isabel Mussi. By the early months of 1932, members of the Balham Group were again engaged in an argument with the party leadership over the Central Committee's 'January resolution'. And by then, a few of us were in touch with the American Left Opposition, receiving its publications and talking over Left Opposition's criticisms of the Comintern and the Russian party leadership.

3

Up to 1931, most British communists had scant knowledge of communist oppositional groups abroad, though the names of many departed and expelled leaders were familiar to us through the Comintern's frequent and abusive references to them – hobgoblins haunting the corridors of the Comintern, constantly being exorcized by incantations in the cabalistic terminology of epigonal Leninism.

Leon Trotsky, however, was known to us by his writings, and was much in the news. Exiled to Alma Ata in 1928, he was deported in 1929 to Turkey. In that year he asked for political asylum in England, the country to which he had travelled in 1902, after his escape from Siberia, to meet Lenin, Martov, Plekhanov, Axelrod and other Russian exiles. Labour Home Secretary J R Clynes rejected the application.[35] During 1930, Trotsky's autobiography was published here,[36] and occasional interviews with him appeared in the newspapers. But that there were organized groups in Europe and America supporting the Left Opposition and Trotsky was unknown to us – until one bright cold spring morning in 1931, I called at the 'Bomb Shop' in Charing Cross Road, to buy some pamphlets and say hullo to old Henderson, who ran it.

Henderson was short, rotund, brusque in manner, with bristling white hair, pointed beard and scarlet tie; his was the only socialist bookshop in the West End. An open-style shop – unusual then – it had been designed and decorated in red and gold and emblazoned with the names of past rebels, by socialist painter Walter Crane. Its defiant name, red doors and window frames, and display of socialist and anarchist publications, incited upper-class louts and their toadies to heave an occasional brick through the full-length plate glass door and windows, to daub blue and white paint on to the red, and sometimes to break in at night and wreck the interior. All this Henderson expected. What provoked him to outbreaks of shouting was the non-political behaviour of boys and lads from the 'buildings for the industrious working classes' which rose several storeys high above the shops in Charing Cross Road. All of us on our way to school kicked over Henderson's dustbins and boxes; and on evenings and Saturdays in summer hit many a sixer through his back windows.

So when, in 1925, grimy and in working overalls, I walked into the shop for the first time to buy a socialist weekly, Henderson glowered at me, recognizing me as an erstwhile dustbin kicker and hitter of sixers, one whose younger brothers were still at it. After I had called regularly for some time. Henderson became affable, clearly seeing me as a brand plucked from the burning, and over the years talked helpfully to me about socialism, anarchism, and the books I ought to read.

On sale in the shop on that later day in 1931 were bundles of two American weeklies – *Labor Action*, run by Jay Lovestone, an expelled 'Rightist'; and *the Militant*, published by the American Left Opposition, with articles in it by Trotsky himself, which appeared the more promising publication. The three or four numbers bought that day were passed round among six or seven of us – and our little world was enlarged. There were others, communists who were working for a reformation of the Comintern and its national sections, for a restoration of inner-party democracy, and an international programme of, not just socialism in one country, but world revolution.

Our first letters to the Americans were merely orders for pamphlets advertised in *the Militant*. But then Henderson's supplies were cut off for not paying the accounts. He explained this to me indignantly, for he made nothing on the few copies he sold, and would be much out of pocket if he posted unsold copies back to America. We wrote to the Americans explaining Henderson's problem, saying how important these isolated sales were, and telling them who and what we were, and what we were trying to do in the party.

The Americans were adamant.[37] In the end we had to order our own copies by post if we wanted to go on reading the paper. More letters were exchanged during the summer; but we made it clear to the Americans that we were not prepared to set up a Left Opposition group in Britain. We went along with them on much, such as the restoration of full inner-party democracy in the national sections, a diminution of Russian command of the Comintern, and a recovery of the communism of the founding fathers. And we were deeply shaken by Trotsky's powerful indictment of Comintern policy in Germany, based as it was on the formula that social democracy and National Socialism were 'varieties of fascism', or, in Stalin's words, 'not opposite poles but neighbours'; by Trotsky's warnings of the disaster that would follow for workers in Germany, Russia and throughout the world if that policy was persisted in; and by his call for a principled united front of the Social Democratic Party and the Communist Party to check and defeat the Nazis. All these things we would raise in the party, and fight for, but as members, not outsiders.

We were reassured by Arne Swabeck's statement that

'the Left Opposition's views are not at all those of splitting the communist movement but of unifying it, naturally expecting every Left Oppositionist to work within the party for our views, endeavouring as much as possible to remain a member of the party without however sacrificing these views'.[38] But in a later letter Swabeck wrote: 'our international secretariat, nevertheless, proposes that some concrete steps should be taken towards organization in a preliminary sense', and added: 'Albert Glotzer . . . youth representative on our national committee . . .' after visiting Trotsky, and the international secretariat, would 'stop over in England for the purpose of being helpful in bringing our various contacts together'.[39]

Another letter told us that Max Shachtman was also coming to England 'to do whatever possible to help towards the formation of a Left Opposition group in England', another from Albert Glotzer, staying at Kadikoy, Turkey with Trotsky, confirmed his intention of visiting England, telling us that 'our task in England is the building of an organization of the Left Opposition.'[40]

Uncomfortably, we felt we were being hurried; that a decision was being thrust upon us. To become a group of the Left Opposition meant expulsion merely for 'conspiracy', for breaking the rules; and in circumstances that would incline our party comrades to condemn us unheard, and allow the party leaders to justify absolute repression of discussion by reference to the fabricated but nevertheless widely circulated and believed slanders against the 'Trotskyists'. We all had ties of comradeship with many party members; the party occupied our waking hours, was our vocation, our social life. Our complete commitment was to the revolutionary party, which for us, at the time, was the Communist Party, however sadly it may have gone awry.

Our opinions had also been sent to Trotsky himself. He wrote, urging that 'the British Left Opposition must begin systematic work. You must establish our staff centre, though a small one. You must build your own publications, even on a modest scale. . . . It is necessary to have a steady, uninterrupted activity, analysis, critic and propaganda. It is necessary to educate our cadres, although in the first stages, few. When, in England, more than elsewhere, communism in a short time can conquer the consciousness of the wide masses, so can conquer within communism, in the same short time, the supremacy of the ideas of the Left Opposition, that is the ideas of Marx and Lenin.'[41]

Trotsky's arguments were reiterated by Albert Glotzer of Chicago when he arrived; and by Max Shachtman of New York – urbane, witty, a theoretician of agility and much experience. Meeting Henry Sara, Stewart Purkis, Billy Williams, Harry Wicks and myself, he took up the theme of setting up an open Left Opposition group. 'Someone,' he said in a discouraging phrase, 'has to go to the altar, someone has to be sacrificed.' The candidates for sacrifice looked at each other but said nothing. We remained unconvinced as to the wisdom of the course suggested, though we did agree that it would be useful to begin the regular publication of a journal. There it was left. We were not yet the British Section of the International Left Opposition; and it was to be several months before we became so.*

From the shadowy world of these obscure little meetings, we came out into the unheeding, bustling, seemingly-invincible world of Britain's rulers, the Britain of the

---

* A letter was received from P Frank of the Left Opposition International Secretariat, dated 9 January 1932, but we do not appear to have established any formal relations with that body – about which we knew little or nothing – for several months.

National government, now strongly in command. The revolutionary hours had passed, the multitudes fallen away in bewilderment or despair. Registered unemployment remained around three million; distress and destitution spread like a medieval plague. Here, indeed, the issues of the day were being debated in action among our fellow-workers.

Labour Party leaders – most of them out of parliament – were denouncing 'MacDonaldism' as the head and fount of all offending, thereby diverting blame for the party's disgrace and defeat from themselves to their former but now departed heroes, MacDonald, Snowden and Thomas.

Five members of the Independent Labour Party (ILP) had been returned to parliament, all intransigents;* they rejected new attempts to curtail their right to speak and vote freely, particularly as those attempts were being made by those who had backed the MacDonald administration and all its villainies, and bawled abuse at the ILPers for refusing to do the same. ILP leaders and members, however, were divided on ILP-Labour Party relationships, and not until July 1932 did an ILP conference vote disaffiliation from the Labour Party by 241 votes to 142.

Politically discredited, few in number, inhibited by a reformist philosophy and by obsequiousness to parliamentary procedures and fetishes, the Labour Party in the House of Commons was impotent to check the government's legislative onslaught on the social services and the unemployed.

* The three ILP-sponsored candidates returned were James Maxton, Dick Wallhead and John McGovern. David Kirkwood and George Buchanan were sponsored by their unions, but refused endorsement by the Labour Party, so they joined the ILP group.

The bright day was done; the aspirations and endeavour of fifty years were in ruins. A shaken movement surveyed the wreckage, and as the survivors of the disaster began picking up the pieces, it was plain to the most election-minded constitutionalist in the ranks that the government and the employers could be resisted only by action in the workshops and in the streets. So, as at the end of the General Strike, it was the men and women of the union branches, trades councils, Labour parties and socialist societies who took up the task of rebuilding the shattered defences of labour and of restoring the movement's morale in renewed struggle against hunger, poverty and oppression. They were busy on labour exchange committees; on relief bodies and councils, fighting countless individual cases of injustice; they set up, through the trades councils, associations of unemployed trade unionists; but they also made public protest on ever-mounting scale.

In hundreds of towns and cities, union and socialist banners were lifted against dark winter skies; there were swirling, turbulent clashes with police, incited by authority to deny rights of procession and to use brutality in doing so. A long steady explanation and action began; a stubborn rearguard action that was after a couple of years to halt the capitalist offensive, and compel the enemy to retreat, and make meagre but encouraging concessions.

The battle had to be local – how could it be otherwise in the absence of a national leadership? the ILP was divided and uncertain, and the CP remained isolated and mistrusted. In the alchemy of a brewing revolutionary situation one vital element had been missing – a revolutionary leadership able to reach the masses.

'The Communist Party', wrote Tom Bell later, 'was still isolated, through neglect of mass work in factories and trade unions. To remedy this a special commission was appointed . . . The results were expressed in the January (1932) Resolution . . .

'Almost immediately, a group of Trotskyists appeared in the South-West district of London (the Balham Group). This group, headed by Groves, Purkis, Sara and Wicks, who had been secretly flirting with the local Independent Labour Party for a time, opened an attack on the central committee . . .'[42]

'Almost immediately' – as though, like Prospero's spirits, we had been conjured out of the air! Tom Bell knew better, of course, for he had been attached to the group for a while, and had, with a companion, attended a few meetings.[43] He found nothing amiss – else we should have heard about it from district and national party officials. Our members were all active in party causes, and group meetings were concerned almost entirely with planning, reporting and discussing these activities. Policy discussions arose from that work, or from documents issued by the district or national leadership. Our 'flirtation' with the local ILP branches during the 1931 crisis and after, was open and public, not secret; and at the time of which Bell was writing we were not an organized group, much less 'Trotskyists'; we were busy and convinced members of a party we still hoped would train, educate and organize a revolutionary leadership among the British working people. But our opposition to the party functionaries hardened as they became more and more openly the pliant creatures of the Russian bureaucracy, and we were increasingly aware that reform of the British party would require also reform of the Comintern.

The Central Committee's 'January Resolution' had been produced because of the Comintern's continued dissatisfaction with the British Communist Party. Not, as some suspected, because the Comintern wanted a revolutionary party and a revolution in Britain, or anywhere else, but because the Comintern, being transformed into a department of the Russian state, a state controlled in the interests of the dominant party caucus by a bureaucracy and a secret police, expected Comintern national sections to serve them, not the interests of the working people.

We, like most communists, had supposed that a successful revolution elsewhere would benefit Russia and its people. So it would, but not necessarily Russia's rulers, whose power would be imperilled by such a revolution, unless they could control it as they now controlled the destiny of Russian people. The thought was no sooner whispered than brushed away – but it was true, though it was to be a long time before most of us would admit it openly, to ourselves or to others.

We went on uncomfortably wearing clothes that no longer fitted us, thinking ourselves as more correctly dressed than the Stalinists; more determined defenders of soviet power, more truly communist. Our doubts were, if not dispelled, at least held in limbo by our respect for Trotsky's brilliant mind, experience and revolutionary integrity; he argued forcefully and with a wealth of Marxist precept and theory that the Russian state owned all land and industry, controlled production, and distribution of wealth, and remained therefore a worker's state, temporarily off-course because of wrong leadership and wrong policies.

It did not convince us deep down in our troubled and uneasy consciences, but it seemed better to let such profound and complex matters lie undisturbed; and to go on shouting that the Soviet Union must be defended – and that revolutionary uprisings in other countries were the best way to do it. We could not hope to escape calumny, but at least we could do battle on issues of our own choosing and so limit the area of misrepresentation and distortion to manageable proportions.

An early reaction to the January resolution was a letter sent to the party secretariat drawing attention to criticism of party policy contained in the letter of 26 August 1931, which was refused publication in the *Daily Worker* on grounds that it contained 'incorrect and unhelpful opinions'. As the January resolution contained similar criticism and admitted the errors in policy, would the secretariat now withdraw its statement?[44] The secretariat would not: 'We are surprised that instead of seeing the Comintern resolution as a guide for future action, you are attempting to utilize it in order to justify your own sectarian and academic tendencies.'[45] We noted the reference to 'Comintern resolution' with interest.

These letters were read to the Balham Group on 4 March. The group – which had discussed the January resolution on three occasions, beginning on 15 January – resolved to put its criticism in resolution form: and at the meeting of 18 March 'a discussion took place on the Central Committee (January) Resolution . . . a resolution drafted by Comrade Groves was agreed unanimously by the group to be sent to the secretariat. The group also agreed that representation be made to the London party committee for an urgent and overdue aggregate.'[46]

The group's resolution was sent on 1 April, the day of fools; in it the group questioned the Central Committee's formulation on the party's activities in the trade unions, which said that the trade union branches must be transformed from organs of class collaboration into organs of class struggle . . . The whole line of the party at the Leeds congress and since has been to maintain that job organization can alone be the unit of 'an organ of class struggle; that the very structure, limited scope, organization, constitution and leadership of the unions make them unsuitable as organs of class struggle.'

The group also pointed out that the two major features of the international situation were not mentioned at all in the resolution – the war in the Far East, and the crisis in Germany, where the Nazis were advancing to power. 'The resolution was drafted at a time when the dangers in the Far East and the approaching crisis in Germany were clearly visible, and it should have set out the tasks of the party in relation to both.'

The group went on to call for a party congress, which was two years and more overdue. 'We regard the amount and extent of the discussion allowed on the resolution to be quite insufficient. In view of the present unsatisfactory state of the party as depicted in the resolution itself, we suggest: full open discussion in the party press as a preliminary to a party congress, the date of which should be fixed without further delay.'[47]

The group's criticism was published in the *Daily Worker* for 14 April, with a reply from the secretariat which ignored the major arguments and accused us of 'under-estimating the trade unions'. At the regular group meeting on the day following publication, the secretariat's answer was discussed, and rejected indignantly by the members as inadequate as a reply and untrue in its accusations against the group.

At an aggregate meeting of South-West local members held in Battersea on 20 April we defended our statement and enlarged our attack on the leadership and its policy. On 12 May, the group drew up its reply to the secretariat, denying accusations of underestimating the importance of work in the unions, and that union branches were, as the Central Committee resolution said, 'organs of class collaboration' or that they could be 'transformed' into 'organs of class struggle', a role for which they were unsuited.

In support of our argument, we quoted R P Dutt's *Labour Monthly* notes, in which he asked, 'Do the trade unions provide the means of mobilising the workers for the present struggle? To say this is to be blind to obvious facts . . . (Could) control of the trade union machine be a means to leading the workers' struggle? No, experience has shown repeatedly that this is nothing less than a constitutional reformist delusion . . . the fighting front of the workers can only be effectively built up in the early struggle at the point of production . . .'[48]

Even more to the point was a statement by Lozovsky, chief of the Russian-based and controlled Red International of Trade Unions: 'That we want to explode the trade union apparatus and destroy it, of that there cannot be the slightest doubt.'[49]

Balham again drew attention to Germany, and the international situation. 'We believe this (a party congress) to be more necessary now than ever before . . . The menace of war which grows in the West and the East demands a party united on the basis of conviction and belief in the line of the party. Only a full, unfettered discussion within the party can make this possible.'[50]

This appeared in the *Daily Worker* but without Lozovsky's words, which had been deleted, and with a condemnatory reply by the secretariat.[51] Though the quote from Lozovsky had been suppressed, the *Daily Worker* published two articles by the Red International chief on trade union apparatus and destroy it, of that there cannot Balham Group!

On 3 May, another aggregate meeting of South-West

local members was held in Battersea, at which district organiser R W Robson, and other party functionaries were present, and spoke. We put forward the Balham resolution, and attacked party policy and leadership. Henry Sara and Harry Wicks were among our spokesmen. A few days afterwards, three of us received letters from the district party office.

Henry Sara was charged with 'supporting the general accusations of the lack of integrity, trickery, cowardice, and stupidity which were levelled against the party leadership by Comrade Groves'. Harry Wicks was accused of supporting 'the remarks of Groves which accused the leadership of the party of trickery, of being opposed to criticism and discussion . . .'

The quotations varied somewhat, for letter number three said 'it is reported that . . . you stated that "the policy which has wrecked this local organization has also wrecked others. Battersea represents the state of the party in other parts of the country . . . it is not better but worse than in January," and for this you blame the "stupidity, hesitation and cowardice of the party leadership in the period of September to December 1931".' The letters asked of us, did we 'maintain these views . . . on the present leadership and policy of the party?'[52]

We replied, rejecting the 'reported' quotations as inaccurate and out of context, and pointed out that our opinions on these matters were set out for all to see in the Balham Group resolutions and related statements.

Reports on the state of the party in several major areas were in the hands of the centre. 'Let these be published in full for discussion in the party press and then we shall be in a position to re-assert our statement or to modify it.'[53]

When the secretariat declared that the Balham resol-

utions were the work of 'one or two well-known sec-
tarians'[54] it was clear to us that they were trying to isolate
some of us from the rest of the group, so that they could
demand our submission to official policy, or expel us. What
the party functionaries did not understand was that the
members were convinced that what was being done was
right, and, in fact, not one was to desert in the hectic two
months that followed.

Our aim, the aim of all, was to battle on and compel
the calling of a party congress and the holding of the pre-
congress discussion that could be expected to go with it;
and in the discussion and at the congress present our criticisms and ideas to the party membership.

But it looked as though the party leaders were defer-
ring announcement of a date for the congress until we had
been subdued or silenced. We renewed our demand for a
congress, while offering a re-phrased resolution paragraph
on trade union policy which we hoped would make our
position clearer, and harder for the leadership to refuse
discussion or distort our viewpoint.[55]

Events were forcing us, however, into further immediate assaults on party and Comintern policy, so jeop-
ardizing our chances of securing a congress. Indeed, our
situation had been rendered the more precarious, for im-
pelled by the alarming situation in Germany, we had
risked the publication during May, of the duplicated
journal *The Communist*, containing Trotsky's 'Germany,
the Key to the International Situation', and the statement
that the British Section of the Left Opposition was now
established.

It was published anonymously and circulated care-
fully and secretly; it was a reluctant, uncertain gesture
indeed, and the response to it was a loud, disconcerting
silence. Not all of us were convinced of the wisdom of it –

but once done there could be no going back on it. We began pressing anew for a party congress, and for educational and agitational activity by the party over the situation in Germany.[56]

In June, Arne Swabeck wrote from New York of *the Communist*, 'naturally we greet its appearance with considerable joy. . . . It is our hope however that you will be able, when the next issue appears, to establish a regular address and give some direction for the revolutionary workers . . . how to get in touch with you'[57]; and, several weeks later, 'It is our hope that you will soon be able to have another issue.'[58]

An address! Whose? We were too closely linked as friends, and as critics of the leadership, for one of us to come out as publisher of *the Communist* without bringing suspicion on all the others. To the affluent Americans we must have seemed reluctant martyrs – but then we were but privates in a tiny isolated unit of the army of world revolution, our armaments pitiable, our provisions scanty. Some of us were held back too by anxiety to make plain to our party comrades that we were fighting for, not against the party; and by the knowledge that whatever support we mustered among them for an inner-party discussion, a congress and policy changes, would disintegrate if the movement appeared to be promoted from the outside, which it certainly had not been.

In those last few months in the life of the Balham Group, its minutes show the members busy on routine party work, but carrying on as well an acrimonious correspondence with the London District Committee and the Party Secretariat, on four issues – on the formulation of trade union policy, an issue we had to put aside when told that no more letters from the group on the subject would be published in the party press;[59] on the party leadership's proposal that the London District Committee should, like the Central Committee no longer be elected by the members but handpicked by an appointed 'commission'; on the absence of any party discussion or campaign on events in Germany; and on the need for the holding of a party congress and a pre-congress discussion.

Among local concerns recorded in the minutes was the problem of unemployed organization and on this, too, we clashed on policy with district and national leadership. Efforts to rejuvenate the local branch of the party-controlled NUWM had come to nothing. The Wandsworth Trades Council had formed an association for unemployed trade unionists, but the party had declared war on such bodies and ordered members to break them up. Bill Pyne, by artful and devious argument, had secured the group's permission to join the association; his reports on it convinced us that we should support it and help make it an effective, fighting organization among the unemployed.[60] The district committee rebuked us for this, and ordered us to bring our members and supporters out of the association and enrol them in the NUWM. The Group ignored this instruction,[61] and the association, backed by the Trades Council, and, before long, led by our members, grew in numbers and influence. Many of the trade unionists we met and worked with then became supporters in the years ahead. Several months afterwards, the party itself reversed its policy of destroying the associations, and ordered members to support them.

The minutes show us maintaining our friendly relations with the local ILP branches, particularly the Clapham branch, whose New Morris Hall was often the venue for our occasional public meetings, socials and conferences. The comradeship which had begun in the autumn of 1931 with such staunch socialists as Sid Kemp and his brother, Alwynne Wynne, and Miriam Knibbs, Ernie Patterson, Harold Ratten, and several others, was to endure until the coming of war scattered us all, and the old days were done.

It was at the New Morris Hall amid the excitements of late 1931 that we met Hugo Dewar. An ILPer for a couple of years or so, he was, in 1931, a member of the Marxist League, a small organization of which none of us had heard, and which revolved around the unusual personality of freelance socialist and secularist, Francis Ridley. Marxist League members had, we learned, been reading and circulating *The Militant*; and Ridley and an Indian member, Chanda Ram, had sent Trotsky a thesis on the theme that 'Great Britain is at the present time in a transitional phase between Democracy and Fascism', to which Trotsky replied at some length in *The Militant*, concluding, 'It would be very sad if the critical members of the British Communist Party would imagine that the opinions of Ridley and Ram represent the opinions of the Left Opposition.'[62] Hugo Dewar had disagreed with the Ridley-Ram thesis, and now linked up with us and the ILP at Clapham in our campaign against the National government's 'economies'; and presently joined the CP, becoming a member of the Tooting Local, linking up as an individual with the Balham Group in its struggle within the party.

The district leadership was uneasy about our collaboration with the ILP, and sharply critical when we joined with the ILP in establishing a committee to organize the May Day demonstration.[63] Because of events in the Far East, we kept the joint committee in existence after May Day, to campaign against 'imperialist war' – Japan's invasion of Manchuria in 1931 had culminated in a successful conquest of the province, and in February 1932, Japan set up there the puppet state of Manchukuo, a base for further military adventures at the expense of China, and maybe of Russia. The Comintern had ordered its sections to mobilize opinion and protest against this plot of the imperialist powers against the Soviet Union, and the CPGB had called for the setting up of anti-war committees; and the campaign shaped itself along the usual lines – the workers' fatherland was in danger, Britain and other imperialist powers were supporting Japanese aggression against Russia and China, and the workers had to take militant action against their imperialist governments; the social democrats, the left socialists and the pacifists had to be exposed as allies of the imperialists. 'Pacifism is the twin ally of the bloodiest imperialism,' wrote R P Dutt, calling for 'neither imperialist patriotism nor pacifism but the active mass fight for the destruction of imperialism and the victory of Socialism.'[64]

Hardly had these words appeared in print when the 'Leninist line' on war was repudiated: a Comintern-backed campaign was launched for a spectacular world congress against war, the public appeal being made by French pacifist Henri Barbusse, and addressed to progressives, liberals, pacifists, as well as to the working classes.

The promptness with which CPGB members obeyed Comintern instructions and jettisoned orthodox Leninist policy on war in favour of attitudes it had always denounced; the fervour and haste with which members argued for the new policy; the sight of comrades we had known and respected for years as principled marxists and devoted communists, distributing an appeal couched in liberal and pacifist terms for a projected world parade of non-revolutionary, anti-revolutionary and most non-socialist notabilities, should have shocked us into looking a little more thoroughly into our own ideas and actions and at the course we had set for ourselves. We did not. Instead, we championed the accepted Leninist position on war. We still believed that such departures from orthodoxy were temporary aberrations from principles shared in common, the correctness of which we had – or would admit to ourselves – no doubt. We were still in the same psychological sphere as the people with whom we were in conflict – our differences, we told ourselves, were limited to certain issues. Even after we had been expelled, and were being ostracized and vilely abused, we continued to believe this; and some remained in that mind, making no reassessment, not looking behind causes to effects, nor wondering what obscure questionings stayed us from the absolute capitulation of so many admired and worthier comrades. When the appeal for the World Congress Against War was launched, and for a British pre-Congress at Bermondsey to precede the greater charade at Amsterdam, we opened what was to be our final campaign as members of the CPGB.

4

In 1932 the ILP organized a national campaign calling for action to stop Japanese aggression. It was the Clapham ILP, therefore, with our agreement, that called an area conference on the subject at the New Morris Hall on 2 July, with Dr C A Smith as chief speaker. Seventy delegates were there from thirty local organizations; at the end of the conference, the organizations represented agreed to elect two delegates apiece to serve regularly on the anti-war committee.[65]

Thus, greatly enlarged in numbers and influence, our small joint committee became the South-West London Anti-War Committee, and was to provide us with a useful base for our work in the area for some time ahead. One of our first moves on the enlarged committee was to propose a series of open-air meetings on the critical German situation – meetings expressing solidarity with the German workers in what we still hoped would be a united stand by Social Democrats and Communists against the advancing Nazis.

For Hitler's National Socialist Workers' Party had advanced in Germany in apparent concert with the Japanese conquest of Manchuria; and by July 1932 the pace of that advance was accelerating alarmingly. From a vote of 810,000 in 1928, the Nazis had climbed to a vote of 6,409,600 in 1930, when the Social Democrats polled 8,577,700 votes, and the Communists, 4,592,000. In the

second stage of the March 1932 presidential election. Adolf
Hitler polled 13,418,500 votes against the Social-Democrat-
supported Hindenburg's 19,360,000, and the Communist
Thaelmann's 3,706,800. In June, street battles began, with
the Nazis, protected by the police, invading working-class
suburbs. A defensive pact between Social Democrats and
Communists could yet influence that result, and rouse the
German workers to battle against the fascists.[66]

Our public meetings were held on Sunday 17 July and
on the following weekend, at Brockwell Park, Battersea
Park, Clapham Common, and Tooting. The speakers were:
Bert Joy, ASW, Pickering, TGWU, W Jordan, Labour Party,
Jimmy Lane, Sid Kemp and W Simmons, ILP, and S
Saclatvala, Stewart Purkis and Reg Groves of the Communist Party.[67] At these meetings, reported the *Daily
Worker*, 'a resolution was passed expressing solidarity with
the German workers in their fight against fascism, and
pointing out that a victory in Germany would intensify the
war situation . . .

'R Groves was the speaker at a meeting on Saturday,
23 July, attended by 300 workers, and Henry Sara spoke on
Clapham Common yesterday morning. At both meetings
resolutions were passed emphasizing that a fascist dictatorship in Germany would seriously affect the position of the
working class of the whole world, and declaring the solidarity of the British workers.'[68]

Our main concern, of course, was the party itself; we
still kept alive a diminishing hope that through it, the
Comintern or the German CP might be persuaded to make
an eleventh-hour offer of an organizational united front
with the Social Democrats against the Nazis. We raised the
German question at the aggregate meeting of London
members in July, and there were bitter exchanges between
our people and party leaders on the platform, but nothing

C

was changed. At the elections eleven days later, the Nazis polled 13,745,800 votes – the Social Democrats 7,959,700, the Communists 5,282,600. It was the peak of Nazi advance – and the bulk of Social-Democrat and Communist supporters still held firm. A united front for common resistance to fascism could yet prevail, but the shadows were lengthening ominously; and soon would come the night. On 9 August, the Balham Group wrote again to the party secretariat, protesting that nothing had been done by the party about Germany, urging the organizing of a national campaign, and ending: 'We would ask the party secretariat to see that the party fulfils its duty to the world revolution.'[69]

Our attack on the World Congress Against War had opened with a letter to the secretariat from the Balham Group, saying that the campaign was 'being conducted around a manifesto drawn up by non-revolutionaries . . . this manifesto has received the support of a number of pacifists and social patriots. Many of the signatories . . . played a treacherous part during the last war; some are confusing the fight to prevent war at the present time and others actually support the social system which makes the war inevitable . . . the present campaign is being substituted for the mobilisation of the workers around the Leninist line against war . . .' Leading party members, the letter went on, had signed the manifesto; and the *Daily Worker* has given unconditional support to the campaign. The party should expose the unsatisfactory contents of the manifesto and mandate its delegates to the World Congress to fight for the Leninist line.[70] We received no answer to this.

On 13 August, the *Daily Worker* carried a report under the headline

Militant mandate for delegate –
attitude towards world congress defined.

At the meeting of the South-West London Anti-War Committee held last Monday (8 August) Comrade Wild of the AEU was elected as the delegate of the committee for the World Anti-War Congress.

The delegate was instructed to 'give full support to any resolution, group or section of congress that stands for the following points:

1 Unmasking of the League of Nations and its pacifist trickery, and the exposure of all capitalist disarmament programmes.

2 Refusal to support capitalist war budgets.

3 To explain that in all wars waged by the capitalists the workers should fight, not for the defence of their country but for the defeat and overthrow of their own ruling class.

4 Development of an agitation amongst the workers for full credit and trading relations with the USSR.

5 Anti-war agitation and the building of revolutionary groups in the war industries and armed forces.

6 Systematic education of the workers in the fact that the USSR is their country, and that the Red Army is their army, ready to do battle on behalf of the workers in any country.

7 At the same time untiring explanation that the only guarantee of victory for the workers of Russia lies in the development of world revolution.'

Comrade Wild was instructed as above, only one vote being cast against and 28 for.

On 16 August, a long article by J R Campbell – headed 'The Anti-War Congress and its tasks – a South-West London resolution that is not militant but mischievous' – said, among other things, that South-West London's resolution needed 'redrafting on the basis of a genuine fight against the plans of the warmongers and the cutting out of the phrases which conceal Trotskyist meanings'.[71]

On the same day, Henry Sara, Harry Wicks and myself were summoned by London organizer R W Robson to district headquarters. When we arrived we found Willie Gallacher, Harry Pollitt and Kay Beauchamp – a well-connected mediocrity – waiting for us. Where, asked Henry Sara, was Robson? He would not be present, was the answer. Henry rose. 'Robson invited me here,' he said, 'and if he is not coming, then I'm not waiting.' And he walked out. It was neatly done, and probably Harry and I should have followed, but we were too surprised to move, and remained to face the inquisitors. Pollitt, startled and annoyed dismissed Henry's act as 'mere liberalism' and turned to us. Would we cease our opposition to party line and leadership particularly on the World Congress Against War? We would not. Gallacher blinked at us over his spectacles – did we realize that we were doing harm to the party? Encouraging sinister forces? 'Some very strange circulars are going round the country', he said. The individual was nothing, the party everything, he went on. To talk about doing our own thinking was petit-bourgeois, and at the word petit-bourgeois, tiny bubbles of saliva began gathering at the corners of his mouth, and his voice became harsher.

Gallacher was personally a kindly and generous man, but certain political phrases seemed to set him off on an uncontrolled torrent of bitter vituperation. Pollitt probably saw the danger signal, for he now interrupted Gallacher to ask again, were we prepared to accept the policy laid down by the Comintern and the party and the discipline of the party? 'Open the pre-congress discussion, Harry,' I said, 'and let it all be settled at party congress.' He waved that away, hesitated, then went abruptly to a table on the other side of the room and picked up a duplicated paper. He brought it near enough for us to see what it was, but not near enough for us to read what it contained, or to be contaminated by it. It was *The Communist*.

'This is the kind of thing that is being circulated among party members – can't you see how dangerous it could be. And it is your opposition that encourages this danger – let me ask you again, Reg and you Harry, will you now help to unite the party by supporting party policy and accepting party discipline?' We stayed silent, knowing that once we gave such assurances we would be asked to disavow our criticisms, confess them as errors, and denounce any who continued in opposition. It had to be complete capitulation.

Taking our silence, rightly, as rejection of his appeal. Pollitt turned away, with a gesture of dismissal. There was no more to be said. Outside, an impatient Henry Sara was pacing up and down on the pavement. He seemed aggrieved that we had not followed him out.

Two days later, we each received a letter from Robson. To me and Harry Wicks. Robson wrote that in view of 'your absolute refusal to state that you accept the policy of the Communist Party and will abide by its discipline . . . the special meeting of the working bureau unanimously decided that you be expelled from membership of the party.'[72] But Henry Sara, wiser than both of us, was only 'suspended' from membership, having avoided answering that decisive question!

His expulsion, of course, followed hard upon. The Balham Group was 'liquidated', but its members were invited to apply individually for re-admission to the party. None capitulated, despite stormy meetings and arguments, and individual appeals. On the Monday following our expulsions the party's pre-congress discussion was opened.

Robson circularized group members inviting them to 'a meeting for comradely discussion with local and district party committee representatives . . . at 17 Defoe Road, Tooting', exhorting them, somewhat ambiguously, 'not to allow any personal relations to stand between their duty to the party and the working class'.[73]

The members went to the meeting, where they were subjected to cajolery and criticism, but all stuck to their opinions. At another meeting of the Tooting Local, addressed by Dave Springhall, a lone Hugo Dewar defended the group's opinions, and was duly expelled.[74] Then individuals were summoned to be interviewed, questioned, argued with, offered retention of their party membership, told all sorts of tales – until the group came together to draw up a letter to the district committee, saying: 'Every member of the group is anxious to retain membership of the party . . . and is willing for discussion between the group and the district to continue. The group, however, is in favour of open discussion before the party members and not . . . of the district committee's method of private discussion with individual members . . . (with) no record kept of what took place. . . . The group is prepared to continue the discussion with the committee as a group and to state its case openly before the party membership either in the press or at aggregate meetings.'[75]

There was no reply to this – the last thing the leadership wanted was open discussion of the issues, particularly as, a few days after the first expulsions, they had opened the pre-congress discussion; so the group issued a cyclostyled statement, *To our comrades in the party from the 'Liquidated' Balham Group*, about the 'liquidation', the individual expulsions, and the issues over which it had come into conflict with the party. This we distributed as widely as our numbers and support permitted. Stewart Purkis had been expelled for 'disruptionist activities and political unreliability', and in September, number two of *The Communist* was published, this time carrying an address, and articles on the expulsions, the World Congress

Against War, and extracts from Trotsky's *Letter to a German Worker*.[76]

The party congress was held in November, conveniently for us, at the Latchmere Baths, Battersea. We painted slogans on walls facing the entrance to the hall; and on the morning congress opened, Harry Wicks and I stood outside on the pavement, distributing *An Appeal to Congress delegates from the Balham Group*, which summarised our views on the trade union question, the united front, the German crisis, party democracy, and the World Congress Against War, ending: 'We seek to return to the party and stand by our comrades in the trials ahead. To this end we ask the congress delegates to raise, inside the congress, the question of our return to the party: to demand access to the documents in which our point of view is set out: to allow one of our members to take part in the congress: and in so doing, help towards building a virile Communist Party, free from the bureaucracy which in the past few years has done so much harm.'

As we stood outside the hall, many party members who knew us scurried past with averted faces; a few showed hostility, and made threatening gestures; others, taken by surprise, accepted our leaflets, only to have them snatched from their hands at the door by William Rust. We saw none refuse his request to hand over the leaflets, not even Wally Tapsell.

The congress and our activities were described as we saw them in a letter to Albert Glotzer, in Chicago:

The party congress took place in the middle of November. We presented a statement to the congress on behalf of the expelled Balham Group, and another statement was presented from the British Group of the Left Opposition. Outside the congress we painted such slogans as Not National Socialism but World Revolution. Reinstate the expelled Left, Release Rakovsky and return Trotsky, and several slogans of a similar character. In spite of threatened violence from party officials we succeeded both in distributing our material and in having delegates inside the congress. We judged it unwise for our delegates in the congress to make any stand since we could not afford to lose valuable party contacts. As it happens, this was justified because the congress was the most docile in the history of the party. The Right wing, principally Hannington and Arthur Horner, were in jail and were removed from the central committee, and the Left wing, as you understand, have been expelled from the party; so that all the resolutions and decisions of the congress were carried with very little argument. Resolutions were carried condemning the Spanish [CP] political bureau and approving their expulsion, and also approving the expulsion of Zinoviev, Kamenev and others, without material or discussion of any kind. A new constitution was approved by the congress, but has not yet actually been published, which allows in future for delegates to the congress to be picked by district committees on the basis of their loyalty to the party line, a condition which is quite a new development in the International...[77]

In the closing speech of the congress, Pollitt said: 'I ask the congress delegates to go away from this congress full of contempt, hatred and loathing for the miserable gang of counter-revolutionaries who, on the walls outside the congress, have written the slogan "Not National Socialism but World Revolution" '. If, he went on, there were any in the congress who supported those 'scoundrels' but who had 'not the courage to express that support . . . if they dare raise their heads inside our movement . . . we will smash and destroy them'.[78]

Pollitt had acquired already the theology, style and vocabulary of Stalinism. Minor and major functionaries, and the basic cadres of the party had to acquire it too; to accustom themselves to perform the rituals of revolutionary struggle, to use the postures and phrases of the revolution, as cover for an expediency and opportunism which served not the workers of the world but the rulers of Russia.

We met many of our old comrades in the months that

followed our expulsion – for these were months of continual agitation, of meetings, marches, demonstrations, of repression and arrests by the increasingly-worried authorities, until even the official movement was shaken into action and full-scale protest. Privately, our old comrades admitted the validity of much that we said, and were apologetic at the abuse being heaped upon us by the party. Publicly, they were silent.

To them the party had become all, greater than the ideas and ideals that had made them rebels and communists, which survived only in set phrases and formal declarations used to gain support for a party and an alien government that were discrediting and destroying those very ideas and ideals. They had, in Ignazio Silone's phrase, 'made relative what should be permanent'. Our fault was that we went on talking like they did for some time after our expulsion; and confined our thinking to those Marxist themes emphasized and restated by a triumphant Leninism and written as dogmas into the life and work of the Comintern. We were not helped in this respect by our having entered the world of international Trotskyism, which was beyond our control and often beyond our understanding. Instead of clearing away political lumber and its jargon, the pronouncements of the International Left Opposition merely added to it.

That we survived as a group the expulsions and the many assaults made on us by the party, was because we had support among the unemployed and trade unionists in South-West London. Frequent attempts were made by the party to oust the 'counter-revolutionary Trotskyists' from the Anti-War Committee; and we were paid a grudging tribute by London party organizer R W Robson when he told his district committee that there was only one representative and active anti-war committee in the whole of London. The principal reason for this was, he was sorry to say, that there were a number of Trotskyists on it.

As the British section, Left Opposition, we were invited to send someone to an enlarged meeting of the Left Opposition's International Secretariat, to be held from 4 to 8 February 1933, in Paris. On 30 January, Hitler had been appointed Chancellor of Germany by President Hindenburg, and it was felt that we ought to send someone to the meeting. A reluctant delegate, I travelled to Paris, and sat through complex, heavily-jargonized discussions in French and German, with someone whispering occasional explanations in English, on Saturday, and again on Sunday, when every so often the proceedings were interrupted by hoots, howls, shouts, screams, the crash of breaking furniture and the thump of falling bodies from the room overhead where the League of French Pacifists was in conference.

That evening, walking through the streets of Paris with aching head and jaded spirits, I saw newspapers being sold on the streets, the newsvendors carrying placards – '250,000 at Hyde Park'. So the movement was on the mend, and even officialdom had been pushed into making an impressive show of strength – indeed, within twelve months the government would be in startled retreat. There was revival, renewal of struggle, but to what end? So that the working people could be sold out by shallow-pated Labour careerists, or duped by Stalinism? There was, too, something unreal in evening retrospect about the Left Opposition conference solemnly pronouncing on those controversies of the Comintern, and even earlier ones of Russian Social Democracy. Hitler and the Nazis stood on the threshold of total power. Surely there could be no true renovation of socialist ideas, or renewal of the forces and spirit of rebellion and resistance, in those old, obscure contentions, argued out again in the thick accents of a now degenerate communism?

Back home – and on 27 February, the monthly delegate meeting of the anti-war committee, and yet another attempt by communists to remove the Trotskyists. They came primed with a suitable resolution; and the final speech in support of it was made by a tall, spare young zealot, Soderland. His shrill tones echo in the memory still, though not, fortunately, most of what he said. His voice rose to a higher pitch of hysteria as he concluded, jabbing a bony, accusing finger at us: 'They even want a united front' – and he screamed the last words – 'with the vile Social Democrats!'

The invaders, who built nothing and destroyed what others built, were repulsed again, their resolution defeated. A small incident, but as was the way of such things, we were elated as we walked home through the chill night air. Well might we have had misgivings had we known how fateful that night was to be:

> *Some consequence yet hanging in the stars.*
> *Shall bitterly begin his fearful date*
> *With this night's revels.*

For on that night, the German Reichstag was set on fire, a dire combustion that was in due course to burn much, much more than Germany's parliament. Immediately, though, the German CP was made illegal, the Nazi terror unleashed, thousands of Social-democrat and Communist officials and members arrested. Consumed in the flames, too, was the disastrous policy imposed by Stalin's men on the German party and the Comintern. The Comintern now called on its sections everywhere to approach the social-democratic parties for a united front. On 8 March, just two weeks after it had ridiculed an ILP suggestion for a united front appeal to TUC and Labour, and nine days after Soderland's speech, the CPGB did just that! Like sponges, the party members squeezed the old policy out of their pores and sucked in the new one.

Too late, of course. On 5 March, amid burnings, beatings, arrests and suppression of socialist and communist meetings and newspapers, Germany went to the polls. Seventeen million votes – 43 per cent of the total – went to the Nazis, the Social Democrats polling 7,182,000, the Communists 4,845,000. On 23 March, Hitler asked parliament for dictatorial powers and got them. The most powerful socialist and communist parties in Western Europe were destroyed without resistance.

If all this made any impression on the Soderlands, it was not visible in their words and deeds. William Gallacher, denouncing the 'ignoramuses of Balham', wrote that, 'a well-known writer who has had considerable association with the revolutionary movement asked me if there was any possibility of a reconciliation between Trotsky and Stalin.

> 'Ask me,' replied Gallacher, 'if there is any chance of Trotsky and Hitler coming together, and I'll think your question worth considering.'
> The writer was horrified and showed it. 'You are not serious,' he said.
> 'I am quite serious', replied Gallacher.[79]

In August 1939, it was Stalin and Hitler who 'came together', in the bloodiest diplomatic handshake in history! And thus the whirligig of time brings in his revenges . . .

References

1. *The Communist*, no.1, May 1932, published anonymously.
2. Issued cyclostyled as *An Open Letter to Harry Pollitt* after the Balham expulsions, 1932.
3. Letter to Reg Groves from the London District Committee of the Communist Party of Great Britain (CPGB), 17 August 1932.
4. London District Party Committee, CPGB, circular to *All Members of the Balham Group*, 17 August 1932.
5. *ibid.*
6. For a useful digest of Russian-Comintern structural and policy changes see Hugo Dewar, 'Communist Parties', in *Marxism, Communism and Western Society. A Comparative Encyclopaedia*, Germany 1971, pp104–12.
7. Leon Trotsky, *The Lessons of October*, translated by Susan Lawrence and I Olshan, London 1925, pp75, 80.
8. CPGB, *The Ninth Congress*, with resolutions of the 7th and 8th Plenums of the ECCI (on Britain), London 1927.
9. *Labour Monthly*, January 1928, pp44–48.
10. Tom Bell, *The British Communist Party*, London 1937, pp125, 135.
11. Allen Hutt, *The Post-War History of the British Working Class*, London 1937, pp192–93. See also, Hutt's review of Bell's book in *Labour Monthly*, June 1937, pp382–86. Dewar has documented a refutation of Hutt's opinions in *Communism in Great Britain*, pp95–97, as yet unpublished.
12. Tyneside District Party Committee, CPGB, *Communist Review*, October 1929, pp568–69.
13. London District Party Committee resolution, *Communist Review*, November 1929, pp610–18.
14. 10th Plenum ECCI, *The World Situation & Economic Struggle*, London nd, pp17, 18. See also, H Pollitt, '10th Plenum Lessons', *Communist Review*, October 1929, pp560–67.
15. Tasks of the CPGB. Statement of the Central Committee, *Communist Review*, September 1929, p520.
16. Letter to R Groves, 27 November 1929.

17. CPGB, *Resolutions of the 11th Congress*, London 1930.
18. H Pollitt, '10th Plenum Lessons', *Communist Review*, October 1929, p567.
19. *Communist Review*, July 1930.
20. Letters: R Groves to Secretariat, 26 February 1930; Daily Worker Editorial Board reply, 24 March 1930.
21. W Rust, 'The Daily Worker', *Communist Review*, June 1930, p258.
22. W Rust, *The Story of the Daily Worker* (ed A Hutt), London 1949, p17: 'On 1 April we introduced the *Worker's Notebook* which became one of our most popular and pungent features and with which the name of William Holmes will always be associated . . .'
23. Letters: R Groves to Secretariat, 22 April 1930 and 14 May 1930; Secretariat's reply 14 May 1930. R Groves to Secretariat and Daily Worker Editorial Board, 30 May 1930; Editorial Board replies 1 June and 22 June 1930; Secretariat's replies 4 June and 8 July 1930.
24. 'A Worker's Notebook', *Daily Worker*, 8 March, 9 March, 22 April, 25 May 1930.
25. *ibid*, 26 April 1930. See also *Communist Review*, April 1930.
26. *Communist Review*, May 1930 and October 1930.
27. F Utley, *Lancashire and the Far East*, London 1931; and Cotton, CPGB London 1928. See also F Utley, *Odyssey of a Liberal*, Washington 1970.
28. S Purkis, 'Danger Ahead', *Labour Monthly*, November 1930, pp668–69.
29. Political Bureau, CPGB, 'The Theoreticians of "Left" Sectarianism and Spontaneity', *Communist Review*, January 1931, pp11–19.
30. J Mahon, 'The Workers' Charter Convention', *Labour Monthly*, May 1931, pp283–86.
31. W Rust, 'The Eleventh Plenum of the ECCI, *Communist Review*, June 1931, p221.
32. R P Dutt, 'The Political Situation and the Fight for the Charter', *Communist Review*, June 1931, p211.
33. P Snowden, An Autobiography, London 1934, p942: 'The only proposal to which the general council were not completely opposed was that the salaries of ministers and judges should be subjected to a cut.'
34. R Groves, Letter, *Daily Worker*, 25 August 1931; Secretariat's reply 27 August 1931. Letters of R Groves of 26 and 27 August not published. For a fuller statement see R Groves, Letter of 15 September 1931 published in the American *Militant*, 10 October 1931.

35. *Manchester Guardian*, 19 July 1929, and *Daily Herald*, 22 July and 25 July 1929.
36. Leon Trotsky, *My Life*, London 1930.
37. Arne Swabeck to R Groves, 8 August 1931. Earlier letters have not survived.
38. *ibid*, 29 September 1931.
39. *ibid*, 29 September 1931.
40. *ibid*, 26 October 1931.
41. Trotsky, letter to R Groves, 27 October 1931.
42. Tom Bell, *The British Communist Party*, London 1937, p150.
43. There are fleeting references to Bell in the Rail group minutes but he seems to have faded away after a time. See p11 and p27 for references to his absence.
44. Letter: R Groves to Secretariat, nd.
45. Letter: Secretariat to R Groves, 29 February 1932.
46. Balham Group minutes, p60.
47. Letter: Balham Group to Secretariat, 1 April 1932.
48. R P Dutt, *Labour Monthly*, February 1932, pp76–78.
49. A Lozovsky, *RILU Magazine*, 15 February 1932.
50. Letter: Balham Group to Secretariat, 12 May 1932.
51. *Daily Worker*, 27 May 1932.
52. Letters: District Committee to R Groves, H Wicks, H Sara, 31 May 1932.
54. *Daily Worker*, 10 June 1932.
55. Balham Group minutes, 10 June 1932, p91.
56. Letter to Secretariat, 13 June 1932; Secretary's reply 24 June 1932. 'Central Committee resolutions', we were told, 'are circulated for discussion and carrying out, not for reformulation by party units.'
57. Arne Swabeck to R. Groves, 8 June 1932.
58. Arne Swabeck to H Sara and R Groves, 25 July 1932.
59. Balham Group minutes, 28 June 1932.
60. *ibid*, 8 April 1932.
61. *ibid*, 15 April 1932.
62. *Militant*, 12 December 1931.
63. Balham Group minutes, p86 (13 May 1932) and p88 (nd but presumably 3 June 1932).
64. *Labour Monthly*, May 1932, pp267, 268.
65. *Daily Worker*, 4 July 1932.
66. For Trotsky's writings on fascism in Germany see Leon Trotsky, *The Struggle Against Fascism in Germany*, Pathfinder Press New York 1971.
67. *Daily Worker*, 16 July 1932.
68. *ibid*, 22 and 25 July 1932.
69. Balham Group to Secretariat, 9 August 1932.

70. *ibid*, 23 July 1932.
71. *Daily Worker*, 16 August 1932.
72. R W Robson to R Groves, 17 August 1932.
73. R W Robson to Balham Group members (circular), 17 August 1932.
74. Hugo Dewar has written two studies of Russian repression of oppositionists – *Assassins at Large*, London 1951, and *The Modern Inquisition*, London 1953 – and an unpublished history of the CPGB.
75. Balham Group to District Committee, 4 September 1932.
76. Eight numbers of *The Communist* were published between May 1932 and May 1933, when the printed *Red Flag* commenced.
77. R Groves to A Glotzer, 7 January 1933.
78. CPGB, *The Road to Victory*, London 1933, quoted in *The Communist*, no. 4.
79. William Gallacher, *Pensioners of Capitalism*, London nd, p3.

Documents

TO OUR COMRADES IN THE COMMUNIST PARTY FROM THE "LIQUIDATED" BALHAM GROUP.

Dear Comrades,

"No other party or working class organization provides such opportunity of full free and open discussion by all workers". With these words the Party pre-congress discussion was opened in last Monday's *Daily Worker*.

Two days later the London District Party Committee "liquidated" the Balham Group; expelled Reg Groves and Harry Wicks, and suspended Henry Sara. The principal charge against the group and against these comrades is that of *"opposing the line of the Party in relation to the World Anti-War Congress"*.

As part of our group work we have discussed such vital issues as the German position, the anti-war campaign and the state of our Party: we have reached conclusions and fought for them as a group. We have for some long time, urged the opening of a Party discussion and the holding of the long overdue Party Congress. Now that the discussion has been opened, and the Party Congress fixed for October, the Balham Group has been "liquidated", and its leading members expelled and suspended.

What a contrast of words with deeds! Reassuring

phrases about "full free and open discussion", but drastic action against those who advance serious criticism of the Party's policy. The great tradition of Bolshevism, the method of Lenin – that of open discussion preceding party decision – is being replaced by orders from above, phrase-mouthing and bureaucratic stifling of criticism. Bureaucracy has already weakened our Party: if persisted in it will smother real Congress discussion, and prevent our party achieving the clarity necessary for struggle.

On our position to the World Anti-War Congress we stand firm. There is danger of a new world war: the lives of millions are at stake. Full and serious consideration of every stage of the struggle against war is imperative. Yet the criticism of the Congress advanced by this group has been refused publication, and even our right to voice such criticism denied. Because we maintain this right they attempt to drive us from the Party.

This World Anti-War Congress has been convened by Barbusse: = the advocate of fusion between Amsterdam and the Comintern, and Rolland; the [indecipherable] devotee of Ghandi. Around these two have gathered intellectuals, pacifists and left socialists the parlour defenders of the U.S.S.R. To seek allies among the most sincere and courageous of the petty bourgeois pacifists is one thing: *to entrust to them the leadership of the struggle against war, is quite another. Yet this is what Pollitt by signing the manifesto, has declared the Party agrees to do.* Our group holds that the first task of the Party is to build the workers united front against war; for upon the international proletariat rests the defence of the U.S.S.R. A world anti-war congress must be a workers congress initiated by the Comintern with the aim of bringing to our side the masses of the workers now organized under the banner of the Second International. But the present Congress is based upon a united front from the top, on a pacifist slogan of 'resistance to war'.

For this anti-war campaign our Party are distributing, not the message of Lenin but the Rolland-Barbusse appeal. The messages of these two conveners of the Congress invoking the aid of all classes – this pacifist poison-gas – is distributed to workers by Communists all over Britain. Congress social-patriots are given advertisement as genuine anti-war fighters: and new victims are thus taught to trust old and proved traitors. Pollitt appears united with Maude Royden and all the other peace time war resisters. For the sake of "unity" with pacifists, careerists, humbugs, and politicians, Lenin's way of fighting war is pushed out of sight. For appealing to Lenin's method against Rolland and Barbusse at this time, on the eve of war, the Balham Group is liquidated and its point of view suppressed.

While this criminal farce at Amsterdam is described as the fight against war, the actual danger of war grows greater. The growth of Fascism in Germany, menaces the existence of the Party and the workers organizations and brings Germany near to the anti-Soviet bloc. *What happens in Germany will decide for years ahead the fate of the European workers.* Our group discussed the German situation, organized, through the local anti-war committee, solidarity meetings: demanded a discussion throughout the Party, and a wide campaign amongst British workers. But the Party remained silent on the German events. Not until the von Papen coup d'état in July did the Party move; and then it only hurriedly organized week-end meetings. Even to-day, the Party fails to respond to the march of events in Germany. There are still no leaflets, no pamphlets, no solidarity meetings on this question.

On these and other issues we feel that we are justified in breaking the ban on real discussion. The falling Party membership, the declining *Daily Worker* circulation, the absence of Minority Movement influence, proves a real discussion to be imperative. By discussion we mean, not formal acknowledgements of the correctness of the Party line, but a critical examination of the line, and particularly of its operation during the latter part of 1931. We hold that wrong Party policy and bureaucracy in the Party are responsible for its unsatisfactory position.

Unless we give up our point of view, we are threatened with expulsion. But we joined the Party believing it to be the only Party for the workers; we still think this, and we shall hold both to our point of view and to the Party. We shall not be harassed, as was Murphy, into deserting the Party. We shall work to win the membership to our point of view. Expulsions and "liquidations" will not be the last word in this struggle. We shall fight within the Party for re-instatement, we shall appeal to the Central Committee, to the Party Congress, to the Comintern. Meanwhile we shall constantly put before the Party our criticisms and suggestions, and shall – in this area – keep on working for Communism and for the Party, side by side with all other Party members.

We do not want to return in order to "vote and keep quiet", we want to play our part in the struggle against wrong policy, against bureaucracy, and for the correct policy essential for Communist work for the revolution.

Only by struggle can the Party be changed from a paper-distributing, phrase-mounting, resolution-passing machine, into a live and vigorous section of the International. We want to help with this job. We ask you, comrades, to demand our re-instatement as a group.

We are, comrades, yours fraternally,

THE BALHAM GROUP.

Steve Dowdall	11 years membership.	
Harry Wicks	11 ,,	,,
Henry Sara	9 ,,	,,
Jim Barratt	8 ,,	,,
D. Groves	6 ,,	,,
Reg. Groves	5 ,,	,,
W. Pyne	9 months	,,
F. Chalcroft	8 ,,	,,
I. Mussi	8 ,,	,,
C. Whiting	8 ,,	,,
M. Simmonds	8 ,,	,,
N. Dowdall	6 years	,,

The Secretary, The Balham Group, C.P.G.B. 68 Childebert Road, London, S.W.17.

An Open Letter to Harry Pollitt: General Secretary of the Communist Party of Great Britain.

Dear Comrade Pollitt,

You have asked a straight question: you have a straight answer. You have asked me how far I go with *The Communist:* the bulletin which contained Comrade Trotsky's article "Germany: the key to the International Situation", and other material by the British Group of the Left Opposition. My answer to you and my comrades in the British Party is: "I go with it all the way". Not only does this answer inevitably incur expulsion: it also entails misunderstanding, disappointment and condemnation amongst valued comrades. It is my duty to them and to the Party, that I state clearly why I take my stand with the British Group of the Left Opposition.

First I wish to say that my reasons are political not personal. During my five years of Party membership, I have experienced – with few and trifling exceptions – nothing but goodwill and comradeship in my Party life: the rank and file of the Party are, as a whole, splendid comrades and fellow workers. The leadership of our Party has in it men of outstanding gifts: a writer as acute as R. P. Dutt; an organizer as skilled as Emile Burns; a speaker, tactician and mass leader as able as Harry Pollitt. Such is the character of the rank and file: such is the quality of the leadership.

This is my estimate of our Party and its leadership. I state it, that it may be clear that it is not because of unsatisfactory personal relationships with the rank and file, not because I underestimate the ability and gifts of its leadership that I line up with the Left Opposition. I support the Left Opposition because I believe that the *policy* of the British Party and of the Communist International is at fault on those very root issues for which Comrades Trotsky, Rakovsky and the many comrades of the Left Opposition have fought and have been expelled.

The very facts I have indicated: the gifted leadership of the British Party, the comradely and industrious rank and file, the developed objective conditions – all these contrast so vividly with the Party's failure to win the leadership of the British working class, that every Communist has it as his plain duty to ask himself whether the Party is on the correct line. The position in Britain to-day, after ten years of hard struggle is: 1. *Parliamentary:* 70,000 votes for the defence of the USSR: 2. *Industrial:* no roots in factories or trade unions: 3. *Political:* complete failure to make the revolutionary way out plain to the workers. This position repeats itself in the Communist Parties throughout the world. These facts have moved me to accept the Left Opposition criticism of the strategy of the Communist International.

At the time of the Left Opposition struggle and the expulsion of Comrade Trotsky, I was a new member of the Party. Even then it was difficult for me not to oppose the contention that Trotsky, who had shared the leadership with Lenin, who – in the words of Stalin: "had the immediate direction of the practical organization of the uprising" and to whom "the Party was first and foremost indebted for the garrison's prompt going over to the Soviet" could be the "counter-revolutionary" into which Party calumny slowly pictured him. Literature was sparse. The Party's little great men: the Arnots, the Ernie Browns, the Murphys. They said their say: one remained unconvinced but ill-equipped and so refrained from voting. With others I worked on in the Party and continued to study the issues raised by the Left Opposition.

The literature has come slowly to hand. On the past issues: Poland, China, Russian industrial and agricultural development, the Anglo-Russian Committee, all the evidence I have secured justifies the Left Opposition and condemns the line of the Communist International. But though the Left Opposition has been correct, it seemed inadvisable to risk expulsion from the Party, even to take part in a fight to win the re-admission to the Communist International of comrades whose past line had been the correct one. Past issues were past. One turned to the work which clamoured to be done at every depôt gate and street corner.

Then hard on the heels of the disturbing attitude of the Communist International towards the Spanish Revolution, came the crucial issue of Germany. Party comrades "in the know" whispered that the Fascists were to take power unchallenged. German industry is so important to the success of the Five Year Plan, that nothing must disturb the relations between German Capitalism and Russian Socialism. The Five Year Plans were to be completed with the help of German industry: whatever the government!

But Comrade Trotsky's writing on the German issue, especially *Germany: the key to the International Situation:*

the *Letter to a German Comrade* and *What Next?* have vividly shown the position in Europe. They have made it clear that "Who wins in Germany wins in Europe". They have presented the danger of war on the U.S.S.R., not as an annual August shibboleth, but as a living reality.

In 1930 Trotsky warned the Party that their forecasts of the early collapse of Fascism were not justified. Twelve months ago, Trotsky pointed to the United Front of the Communist and Social Democratic organizations as the only policy which could ensure the defeat of Fascism, the break-up of Social Democracy, and success in the struggle for proletarian power. To-day events tardily compel the Party towards Trotsky's line. But time in this struggle is the life and death factor. The line which Trotsky pointed out two years ago, the Party begins to shuffle towards to-day. These delays and weaknesses of both the Communist International and the German leadership threaten disaster to the U.S.S.R. and to the whole working class movement. In the present situation it is to me a clear duty to put Comrade Trotsky's writings in the hands of the Party membership, that his leadership may be available to the working class in this hour of need. That is why I support the work of the Left Opposition in issuing the bulletin for circulating in the Party and to militant workers.

When I was expelled from the Railway Clerks Association, the RCA leadership saw and condemned my action as a "breach of rule". Many of my fellow members and my comrades in the Party saw and supported my action as the course which loyalty to the working class demanded.

I know that I may now be condemned by you and by many valued comrades for breaking rules by circulating this material on Germany. But we who do this hold that loyalty to the Party's cause is more important than keeping rules which ban vital discussion in the Party.

In this short letter I cannot set out the Left Opposition case on the major political issue: the case for the policy of International Revolution against National Socialism (even when it wears the guise of "Socialism in one country! "): and all tactical issues which follow from it. I ask every comrade who sees the importance of mastering these issues to write to me for details of the publications of the Left Opposition.

I write this letter to make it clear that my course of action is dictated by political and not personal motives: and that if my acceptance of the Left Opposition position and support for its works entails my expulsion, I shall from without the Party do my utmost – together with my Left Opposition comrades within the Party – to strengthen the Party for its real task: the organization of the working class for the world struggle for world socialism.

With communist greetings,

Stewart Purkis.

4, HOGARTH HILL, HENDON, LONDON NW11.   JULY 27th 1932.

An Appeal to Congress Delegates
from the Balham Group.

As the Congress discussion opened, leading members of our group were expelled: the expulsions followed a long discussion between the Group and the Party leadership. A few weeks later, nine other members of the Group, because we continued to work as a group, were said to have placed themselves outside the Party. Thus, in S.W. London alone, fourteen active Party comrades have been forced out of the Party.

No explanation of these events appeared in the Party press. The Party leadership gave no reasons to the membership for its actions. Our letters and resolutions to the Secretariat have been kept from the Party. Even the right of appeal, given to every expelled member, has been denied us. Untrue statements circulate to meet any doubts in the minds of those Party members who know of the struggle in this area. Otherwise – silence.

A leadership that suppresses the point of view of its critics is afraid of open discussion. A leadership that refuses to explain measures taken against its critics has a weak case. Our Group has nothing to fear from open discussion. We have fought all along for the thrashing out of differences before the whole Party.

Our criticism of the trade union policy outlined by the C.C. Resolution of January, was made because behind its vague formulations, was concealed the point of view now openly expressed by Pollitt and Gallacher. In reply, we were said to be against work in the trade unions when actually many of our members were more active in the unions than most of the C.C. We were told we were "quibbling". Yet the Party discussion has revealed acute differences within the leadership on this question, and has found R. P. Dutt defending a point of view very close to ours. Dutt and Rust have been accused, as we were, of advocating a course which would throw the Party back "once again into the morass of sectarianism". The delegates cannot fail to see the conflict existing within the leadership on this question. Why then was the Balham Group "quibbling" in raising this question seven months ago?

By approaching local working class organizations in S.W. London, we sought to establish a real united front, in place of the "united front" of the past, which usually consisted of party auxiliaries. We secured such a united front on the basis of the immediate issues affecting the workers. The 12th plenum declared that more proletarian democracy was needed within united front organizations. One of our "crimes" was to put this into practice before the Plenum was held! Why are we refused the right to state our viewpoint on this vital Question?

Overshadowing these questions is the German crisis, and the Balham Group's effort to raise the subject within the party. During the German crisis of 1923, all sections of the C.I. conducted a great campaign. How much has the party done in the last twelve months? Up to the time of our expulsion, we demanded that the party leadership should commence a discussion within the party and conduct a solidarity campaign among the workers. Nothing was done. The party has avoided facing the most serious aspect of the international situation. So much so, that the manifesto of the Amsterdam Congress, contains not one word about Germany. Do the party leaders attach importance to the German revolution? Have we any part to play in that struggle now? Or are they silent in the interests of socialism in one country? Events are showing that our demands were justified. We ask the delegates to the Party Congress to demand that an effective campaign be begun at once.

According to the London D.P.C. our chief "crime" was the carrying, on the S.W. London Anti-War Committee, of a mandate for this committee's delegate to the Amsterdam Congress. The mandate contained, and this was the main objection, the statement that we should tell the workers that the U.S.S.R. was their country, and that the Red Army was their army, ready to fight on behalf of the workers of any country. This elementary statement of the principles of the Russian Revolution was described as "Trotskyism". Yet if this is against the present policy of the Party, the Party has travelled a long way from its position when Lenin led the Comintern.

Our expulsion is a blow at the principles of the Party. By all the tests of Bolshevik criticism, the present party leadership has failed to build the party or its influence in the working class, at a time when opportunities are greatest. Every phase of party experience should have been examined in the party discussion: the memberships should have secured from the discussion Bolshevik understanding and appreciation of the tasks ahead. But open discussion and party education have been replaced by bureaucratic control, drastic misuse of party discipline against critics, the glossing over of vital differences within the leadership, the suppression of vital documents, and in place of argument, invective.

Since our expulsion, we have continued to work to win the workers to a revolutionary point of view. By work in the unions, amongst the unemployed, in the united front, our members have proved themselves active in the struggle. We seek to return to the party and stand by our comrades in the trials ahead. To this end we ask the Congress delegates to raise inside the Congress, the question of our return to the Party: to demand access to the documents in which our point of view is set out: to allow one of our members to take part in the Congress: and in so doing, help towards building a virile Communist Party, free from the bureaucracy, which in the past few years has done so much harm.

The Balham Group

Harry Wicks	11	years membership.
Henry Sara	9	,, ,,
Reg. Groves	5	,, ,,
D. Groves	6	,, ,,
J. Barrett	9	,, ,,
H. Dewar	1	,, ,,
M. Simmonds	1	,, ,,
F. Chalcroft	1	,, ,,
C. Whiting	1	,, ,,
B. Pyne	1	,, ,,
T. March	1	,, ,,
N. Dowdall	6	,, ,,
S. Dowdall	11	,, ,,

To the Delegates to the Party Congress
Battersea, November 1932
From the British Group of
The Left Opposition of the C.I.

Nov. 7th, 1932.

Comrades,

With this letter, we also bring to your notice on this fifteenth anniversary of the October Revolution, copies of two other letters. One from Petrograd, dated Oct. 25th, 1917: the other from Prinkipo, its writer lives there in exile.

We also remind you of the life stories of a past and present U.S.S.R. ambassador to Britain. One, for forty years a revolutionary fighter, Comrade Rakovsky: the other, a deserter from the Mensheviks to Kornilov in 1917 and an opponent of the Bolsheviks till the complete defeat of Koltchak in 1919, the ex-white, Maisky. Comrade Rakovsky, the red fighter of 1892–1932, is now sentenced by Stalinist judges to a renewed term of imprisonment as a bolshevik-leninist: Maisky, the white of 1917–1919, in this fifteenth anniversary, dined at the Lord Mayor's banquet as the diplomatic representative of the U.S.S.R.

The bureaucracy of the Russian Party has jailed hundreds of bolshevik-leninists. It now expels its right opposition, WITHOUT DISCUSSION. Two of Stalin's trio – Kamenev and Zinoviev – go out, WITHOUT DISCUSSION. The German Party's Stalinist theoretician, Neumann, is deposed WITHOUT DISCUSSION. The Stalinist P.B. of the Spanish Party is expelled, WITHOUT DISCUSSION. These events show that democratic centralism has become bureaucracy.

The Left Opposition's line on Germany, Spain and China: its attitude on the United Front, trade union work, and 'workers and peasant organization': its attack on bureaucracy in the Party and the C.I., its proposals on Soviet economy, are surely confirmed as fact piles upon fact. Read our literature. Face the facts.

Restore party discussion at this Congress and in the locals. Work against the sham red united front, for a real, unfettered, united front of working class organizations. Oppose the policy of trusting anti-war mobilisation to the pacifists, intellectuals and adventurers of Amsterdam; defeat those who fear to make definite fighting agreements with the international organizations of the working class. Stand against 'worker and peasant' adventures in colonial policy, for revolutionary, proletarian political organization. Replace party bureaucracy by party democracy. Reject national socialism, take up the struggle for world revolution.

Re-admit to the Communist International those expelled for membership of the Left Opposition.

Communist greetings,

The British Group of the Left Opposition of the C.I.

PETROGRAD LETTER, 1917.

The provisional government is deposed. Power has passed into the hands of the organ of the Petrograd Soviet of Workers and Soldiers Deputies, the Revolutionary Military Committee, which stands at the head of the proletariat and garrison of Petrograd.

The cause for which the people were fighting: immediate offer of a democratic peace, abolition of landlord property rights over the land, workers control over production, creation of a Soviet Government – that cause is securely achieved.

Long live the revolution of workers, soldiers and peasants!

Military Revolutionary Committee,
Petrograd Soviet of Workers and Soldiers Deputies.

Chairman. L. TROTSKY
Petrograd, October 25th (7.X1) 1917. 10 am.

PRINKIPO LETTER, 1932.

The still isolated October Revolution now completes its fifteenth year. This simple figure witnesses to the whole world the gigantic strength native to the one proletarian state. No one of us, not even the most optimistic, had foreseen such enduring vitality. But that is not astonishing: since optimism regarding an isolated proletarian state would entail pessimism towards the international revolution.

Leaders and masses saw the October Revolution as but the first stage of the world revolution. In the year 1917, the idea of independently building socialism in isolated

D

Russia, was neither formulated, advanced, nor defended by anyone. In the following years also, the economic up-building was regarded, by the whole of the Party without exception, as the process of constructing a material foundation to the proletarian dictatorship: as making secure the economic alliance (smyohka) between town and country; and, finally, as the provision of points of support for the future socialist society, which could be built only upon an international basis.

The path of the world revolution has proved immeasurably longer and more devious than, fifteen years ago, we had hoped and expected. To the external difficulties (of which the historic role of reformism has shown itself as the most important) internal difficulties allied themselves: above all the policy, false in its foundations and fatal in its consequences, of the unworthy successors of the October 1917 leadership. The bureaucracy of the first workers' state – unknowingly, but none the less decisively – hinders the bringing into existence of the second workers' state. The bureaucratic knot must be untied or cut to release the advance to world revolution.

Though the dates of development have not kept within the outlines of perspectives set out by us, we had, however, accurately estimated the fundamental motive-forces, and their laws. This also applies completely to the problem of the economic development of Soviet Russia. Modern productive forces cannot be locked within national confines by resolutions or incantations. National self-sufficiency is an ideal of Hitler, but not of Marx nor of Lenin. Socialism and national isolation are mutually exclusive. To-day, as fifteen years ago, the programme of a socialist society within one country is utopian and reactionary.

The economic successes of the Soviet Union are very great. But precisely at this fifteenth anniversary the antagonisms and the difficulties have reached a menacing acuteness. Uneven development, backwardness, disproportions, non-fulfilment of plans speak first and foremost: of wrong leadership. But not only of that. They also warn us that the building of an harmonious society is possible only by an unbroken series of experiments over a course of decades: and not otherwise than upon an international basis. The technical and cultural obstacles, the breach between town and country, the import and export difficulties – all testify to the fact that the October Revolution demands its continuation internationally. Internationalism is not a ritual usage; it is a matter of life or death.

There will be no lack of anniversary speeches and articles. The majority of them will come from those who, in October 1917, were irreconcilable adversaries of the proletarian revolution. By these gentlemen, we, bolshevik-leninists, shall be termed 'counter-revolutionaries'. It is not the first time that History has allowed herself such jokes, and we are not angry with her for that. For, all the same, even if with confusion and slowness, she nevertheless does her work.

And we shall do ours!

PRINKIPO. Oct. 13th 1932.   L. TROTSKY.

For literature, information on the case for the Left Opposition etc, write to STEWART PURKIS, 4 Hogarth Hill, Hendon N.W.11.

GERMANY!

TO ALL COMMUNISTS
AND MILITANT WORKERS

IN GERMANY EVENTS MOVE SWIFTLY TO DE-
CISION. Hitler has become Chancellor and prepares for
absolute dictatorship by suppressing Communist and
Socialist newspapers, prohibiting workers' demonstrations,
weeding out the non-fascists in the state forces, and attach-
ing his own Storm Troops to these forces. Fascism moves
relentlessly on over the bodies of the most devoted German
revolutionaries. With the advance of Fascism to power, the
forces of reaction grow stronger the world over; step by
step with Hitler's advance goes Japan's war offensive.
Within the near future the fate of the German Workers,
of the Communist International, of the Soviet Union, of
the World Revolution, will be decided for many years
ahead. It is time to sound the alarm.

FASCISM IS THE FINAL WEAPON OF FINANCE
CAPITALISM. The bourgeoisie can no longer rule
in the old way: the political crisis in Germany cannot
be solved by the methods of parliamentary democracy. The
bourgeoisie seek to maintain their domination and to over-
come the crisis by scrapping parliament, by abandoning its
old tool, Social Democracy, and using the weapon of

Fascist terror. Since the employers cannot rule by themselves, they enlist petty bourgeois in the armies of Hitler.

FASCISM ANNOUNCES ITS PROGRAMME – "the extermination of Marxism." Italy shows only too clearly what this means. Fascism rules by destroying every independent organization of the masses, recapturing every foothold won by the workers in capitalist society. The Communist and Social Democratic Parties, Trade Unions, Co-operatives, the right to hold meetings, to publish, to organize – these things cannot exist under a Fascist dictatorship. To get victory, the Fascists will engage in a ruthless campaign of murder and destruction, the murder of thousands of the best German fighters, the jailing of tens of thousands, and the forcible suppression of their organizations. Can it be doubted that the defeat of the German Communist Party and of the powerful German working class movement by the motley bands of Hitler, would deal a fatal blow at the prestige and strength of the Communist International?

AND – AT THE SOVIET UNION! For, despite the theory that socialism can be built in Russia independently of the rest of the world, the real strength and ultimate guarantee of socialism in Russia, lies in development of world revolution. A Fascist Germany would attempt the extermination of Marxism outside as well as inside Germany. The ruling class of Germany has nothing to lose and everything to gain by war. Their newly militarised man-power would be placed in the service of France and Britain against the Soviet Union. A Fascist Germany would make war on Russia.

TWELVE MONTHS AGO WE SOUNDED THE ALARM, pointing to Germany as the key to the international situation. We published the writings of Trotsky, in which he pointed out the gravity of the German situation and how much depended on the defeat of Hitler. These warnings were not heeded: for publishing them we were expelled from the Communist Party. If Hitler wins, the responsibility for his victory will rest upon the shoulders of the present leaders of the Communist International and their puppet Central Committee in Berlin. We give below some points in the German Party's policy which have seriously weakened the revolutionary movement.

THE PARTY'S ESTIMATION OF FASCISM. The Social Democrats were called "Social-Fascist". The idea that their government was the "lesser evil" was attacked vehemently. It was said "A Social Democratic coalition government . . . would be a thousand times greater evil than an open Fascist dictatorship", (*Der Propagandst*, Sept. 31.) They spoke of "the beginning of Fascist rule in Germany" (*Rote Fahne*, 17/1/31.) in connection with the Social Democratic government. For them, the Bruening government was Fascist; the Schleicher government was "Fascist". In this way did the C.I. leadership analyze Fascism. Far from seeking, as a Fascist government must, the destruction of the working class forces, these governments actually based themselves on the balanced conflict between the workers movement and the Nazis. But the German Party, tutored by Stalin, taught the workers to see no difference between Bruening and Hitler. If there is already a Fascist government in power, why worry about Hitler? This is the logical deduction many workers have made from Thaelmann's analysis of the differences between Bruening and Hitler.

THE UNITED FRONT. The German Party, following the C.I. policy of the "Red United front", refused to effect a real united front against Hitler. ("A bloc or even an alliance, or even a temporary joint operation, in individual actions between the Communist Party and the Social Democratic Party in Germany against National Socialism would forever discredit the Communist Party'. W. Munzenberg 1/2/32). The social democratic workers were told, in effect, "we will unite with you, but not with your leaders, repudiate them, follow our policy, and we will unite against Fascism". Such a policy made a united front impossible. We refer our Communist comrades to the Theses of the 3rd and 4th Comintern Congresses on the United Front, and also to Lenin's letter advocating a united front with Kerensky against Kornilov (see "Preparing for Revolt" pages 9 to 13). If the policy outlined in this letter had been followed, as the Left Opposition advocated as far back as 1931, the advance of Hitler would have been checked, the Social Democrats' influence over large masses of workers would have been broken, and the road to power opened for the German Party. Twice the German Party have, after announcing it as impossible, made approaches to the Social Democratic leaders, but only as a *manoeuvre,* counting on the to be expected refusal. A campaign must be conducted among the Social Democratic workers, urging them to force their leaders into a united front for struggle against Hitler. Without the Social Democratic workers' organizations, Hitler cannot be defeated.

BY THE ABOVE MISTAKEN POLICIES, by their efforts to be more nationalist than the Nazis, (shown in their attempt to substitute "Peoples Revolution" for "Proletarian Revolution", their support for the Referendum, their making of the ending of the Versailles Treaty the chief plank in their programme) the Party leaders have helped to weaken the Party.

WORKER – COMMUNISTS!

We are faced with a disaster as great as that of 1914. But it can be averted. There is still time: the revolution can and must beat Fascism. The forces of a united working class in Germany would be irresistible, would defeat Hitler, and open a new epoch in history. The Stalinist leadership is too deeply compromised to be able to turn quickly and decisively.

Call local and district Party Conferences to discuss the policy followed in Germany, and to plan a serious solidarity campaign in this country. Make the Communist International break its craven silence with which it has met the new crisis. Return to the policy of Lenin. For the United Front of the Communist Party and the Social Democratic Party against Fascism! For a Soviet Germany! For the Soviet States of Europe!

END STALINIST TREACHERY!

FOR THE POLICY OF LENIN AND TROTSKY!

FOR WORLD REVOLUTION!

Issued by the Balham Group: British Section, International Left Opposition.

UNITE!

TO WORKING MEN AND WOMEN IN S.W. LONDON

Comrades,

Nineteen years ago our masters urged us to maim and kill our German brothers. The German employers sent the German workmen to kill their French and English comrades. Out of the bloody shambles of 1914–1918 the rulers of England, of France and of every other country, made enormous profits: but millions of workers were butchered or maimed: those who returned, returned to unemployment and low wages. The Socialist International failed the workers in their hour of need – in spite of its fine words about international solidarity. A disaster as terrible as that of 1914 threatens us all to-day. Over the homes of the European working class hangs the menace of Fascism and of war. Between us and the catastrophe is the mighty army of the German working class.

Who wins in Germany, wins in Europe for many years to come. Hitler and his murder gangs stand on the threshold of power. Fascism is but a weapon in the hands of the bosses. The capitalists can no longer hold down the German workers by the old parliamentary trickery: so they call together and organize landowners' sons, civil servants and clerks. Hitler will rule with his army on behalf of the rich by crushing every kind of working class organization – socialist, as well as communist, co-operative as well as trade union. By murdering the flower of the German working class, holding down the rest by bloody terrorism, banning their newspapers and burning their headquarters, the Fascists will make possible the driving down of the standard of living of the German workers to unheard of depths. And this would be followed by a general attack on the workers' standards throughout Europe.

Hitler's domestic programme is the destruction of the German workers' organizations and the driving down of their standards of living. His foreign policy will be to enlist Germany's man-power in the service of France and Britain against Soviet Russia in return for colonies and loans. Hitler's foreign policy means world war. Already we see how Japan's military offensive moves step by step with Hitler's advance to power. The struggle to stop world war is at the moment focused in Germany.

Within the next few weeks the fate of Soviet Russia, our German comrades and the workers of the whole world, will depend upon the result of the German conflict. Victory for Fascism means the victory for reaction the world over, it means opening the way for world war. But the defeat of Fascism would open the road to a Soviet Germany and a Soviet Europe. By the unity of Socialist and Communist workers in Germany and throughout Europe, the terrible menace of Fascism can be defeated.

TRADE UNIONISTS! SOCIALISTS! CO-OPERATORS! COMMUNISTS!

Demand that the Labour and Socialist International and the Communist International meet together for united working class action. Urge that Social Democrats and Communists join forces in Germany to defeat Hitler. The shameful treachery of 1914 must not be repeated! Deeds not words! Demand proletarian unity against Fascism and against War!

DOWN WITH THE FASCIST MURDERERS!

FOR THE UNITED FRONT AGAINST FASCISM!

FOR THE SOVIET STATES OF EUROPE!

MEETINGS HELD EVERY SUNDAY MORNING AT 11-30. — CLAPHAM COMMON.

Issued by the Balham Group of the International Left Opposition. 79 Bedford Rd, S.W.4.

INDEX